Martyrdom of St. Perpetua and St. Felicity

and other Writings

Tertullian of Carthage

Translated by: R.E. Wallis, S. Thelwall
Edited by: D.P. Curtin

Dalcassian
Publishing
Company

PHILADELPHIA, PA

Martyrdom of St. Perpetua and St. Felicity

'Martyrdom of St. Perpetua and St. Felicity' translated by R.E. Wallis. From Ante-Nicene Fathers, Vol. 3. Edited by Alexander Roberts, James Donaldson, and A. Cleveland Coxe. (Buffalo, NY: Christian Literature Publishing Co., 1885.)

'On Martyrdom' translated by S. Thelwall. From Ante-Nicene Fathers, Vol. 3. Edited by Alexander Roberts, James Donaldson, and A. Cleveland Coxe. (Buffalo, NY: Christian Literature Publishing Co., 1885.)

'On the Veiling of Virgins' translated by S. Thelwall. From Ante-Nicene Fathers, Vol. 4. Edited by Alexander Roberts, James Donaldson, and A. Cleveland Coxe. (Buffalo, NY: Christian Literature Publishing Co., 1885.)

'On the Apparel of Women' translated by S. Thelwall. From Ante-Nicene Fathers, Vol. 4. Edited by Alexander Roberts, James Donaldson, and A. Cleveland Coxe. (Buffalo, NY: Christian Literature Publishing Co., 1885.)

Library of Congress Cataloging-in-Publication Data

Contents

Preface.

If ancient illustrations of faith which both testify to God's grace and tend to man's edification are collected in writing, so that by the perusal of them, as if by the reproduction of the facts, as well God may be honoured, as man may be strengthened; why should not new instances be also collected, that shall be equally suitable for both purposes—if only on the ground that these modern examples will one day become ancient and available for posterity, although in their present time they are esteemed of less authority, by reason of the presumed veneration for antiquity? But let men look to it, if they judge the power of the Holy Spirit to be one, according to the times and seasons; since some things of later date must be esteemed of more account as being nearer to the very last times, in accordance with the exuberance of grace manifested to the final periods determined for the world. For "in the last days, says the Lord, I will pour out of my Spirit upon all flesh; and their sons and their daughters shall prophesy. And upon my servants and my handmaidens will I pour out of my Spirit; and your young men shall see visions, and your old men shall dream dreams." And thus we— who both acknowledge and reverence, even as we do the prophecies, modern visions as equally promised to us, and consider the other powers of the Holy Spirit as an agency of the Church for which also He was sent, administering all gifts in all, even as the Lord distributed to every one as well needfully collect them in writing, as commemorate them in reading to God's glory; that so no weakness or despondency of faith may suppose that the divine grace abode only among the ancients, whether in respect of the condescension that raised up martyrs, or that gave revelations; since God always carries into effect what He has promised, for a testimony to unbelievers, to believers for a benefit. And we therefore, what we have heard and handled, declare also to you, brethren and little children, that as well you who were concerned in these matters may be reminded of them again to the glory of the Lord, as that you who know them by report may have communion with the blessed martyrs, and through them with the Lord Jesus Christ, to whom be glory and honour, for ever and ever. Amen.

Chapter 1.

Argument.— When the Saints Were Apprehended, St. Perpetua Successfully Resisted Her Father's Pleading, Was Baptized with the Others, Was Thrust into a Filthy Dungeon. Anxious About Her Infant, by a Vision Granted to Her, She Understood that Her Martyrdom Would Take Place Very Shortly

1. The young catechumens, Revocatus and his fellow-servant Felicitas, Saturninus and Secundulus, were apprehended. And among them also was Vivia Perpetua, respectably born, liberally educated, a married matron, having a father and mother and two brothers, one of whom, like herself, was a catechumen, and a son an infant at the breast. She herself was about twenty-two years of age. From this point onward she shall herself narrate the whole course of her martyrdom, as she left it described by her own hand and with her own mind.

2. "While" says she, we were still with the persecutors, and my father, for the sake of his affection for me, was persisting in seeking to turn me away, and to cast me down from the faith—'Father,' said I, 'do you see, let us say, this vessel lying here to be a little pitcher, or something else?' And he said, 'I see it to be so.' And I replied to him, 'Can it be called by any other name than what it is?' And he said, 'No.' 'Neither can I call myself anything else than what I am, a Christian.' Then my father, provoked at this saying, threw himself upon me, as if he would tear my eyes out. But he only distressed me, and went away overcome by the devil's arguments. Then, in a few days after I had been without my father, I gave thanks to the Lord; and his absence became a source of consolation to me. In that same interval of a few days we were baptized, and to me the Spirit prescribed that in the water of baptism nothing else was to be sought for bodily endurance. After a few days we are taken into the dungeon, and I was very much afraid, because I had never felt such darkness. O terrible day! O the fierce heat of the shock of the soldiery, because of the crowds! I was very unusually distressed by my anxiety for my infant. There were present there Tertius and Pomponius, the blessed deacons who ministered to us, and had arranged by means of a gratuity that we might be refreshed by being sent out for a few hours into a pleasanter part of the prison. Then going out of the dungeon, all attended to their own wants. I suckled my child, which was now enfeebled with hunger. In my anxiety for it, I addressed my mother and comforted my brother, and commended to their care my son. I was languishing because I had seen them languishing on my account. Such solicitude I suffered for many days, and I obtained for my infant to remain in the dungeon with me; and immediately I grew strong and was relieved from distress and anxiety about my infant; and the dungeon

became to me as it were a palace, so that I preferred being there to being elsewhere.

3. Then my brother said to me, 'My dear sister, you are already in a position of great dignity, and are such that you may ask for a vision, and that it may be made known to you whether this is to result in a passion or an escape.' And I, who knew that I was privileged to converse with the Lord, whose kindnesses I had found to be so great, boldly promised him, and said, 'Tomorrow I will tell you.' And I asked, and this was what was shown me. I saw a golden ladder of marvellous height, reaching up even to heaven, and very narrow, so that persons could only ascend it one by one; and on the sides of the ladder was fixed every kind of iron weapon. There were there swords, lances, hooks, daggers; so that if any one went up carelessly, or not looking upwards, he would be torn to pieces and his flesh would cleave to the iron weapons. And under the ladder itself was crouching a dragon of wonderful size, who lay in wait for those who ascended, and frightened them from the ascent. And Saturus went up first, who had subsequently delivered himself up freely on our account, not having been present at the time that we were taken prisoners. And he attained the top of the ladder, and turned towards me, and said to me, 'Perpetua, I am waiting for you; but be careful that the dragon do not bite you.' And I said, 'In the name of the Lord Jesus Christ, he shall not hurt me.' And from under the ladder itself, as if in fear of me, he slowly lifted up his head; and as I trod upon the first step, I trod upon his head. And I went up, and I saw an immense extent of garden, and in the midst of the garden a white-haired man sitting in the dress of a shepherd, of a large stature, milking sheep; and standing around were many thousand white-robed ones. And he raised his head, and looked upon me, and said to me, 'You are welcome, daughter.' And he called me, and from the cheese as he was milking he gave me as it were a little cake, and I received it with folded hands; and I ate it, and all who stood around said Amen. And at the sound of their voices I was awakened, still tasting a sweetness which I cannot describe. And I immediately related this to my brother, and we understood that it was to be a passion, and we ceased henceforth to have any hope in this world.

Chapter 2.
Argument. Perpetua, When Besieged by Her Father, Comforts Him. When Led with Others to the Tribunal, She Avows Herself a Christian, and is Condemned with the Rest to the Wild Beasts. She Prays for Her Brother Dinocrates, Who Was Dead

1. After a few days there prevailed a report that we should be heard. And then my father came to me from the city, worn out with anxiety. He came up to me, that he might cast me down, saying, 'Have pity my daughter, on my grey

hairs. Have pity on your father, if I am worthy to be called a father by you. If with these hands I have brought you up to this flower of your age, if I have preferred you to all your brothers, do not deliver me up to the scorn of men. Have regard to your brothers, have regard to your mother and your aunt, have regard to your son, who will not be able to live after you. Lay aside your courage, and do not bring us all to destruction; for none of us will speak in freedom if you should suffer anything.' These things said my father in his affection, kissing my hands, and throwing himself at my feet; and with tears he called me not Daughter, but Lady. And I grieved over the grey hairs of my father, that he alone of all my family would not rejoice over my passion. And I comforted him, saying, 'On that scaffold whatever God wills shall happen. For know that we are not placed in our own power, but in that of God.' And he departed from me in sorrow.

2. Another day, while we were at dinner, we were suddenly taken away to be heard, and we arrived at the town-hall. At once the rumour spread through the neighbourhood of the public place, and an immense number of people were gathered together. We mount the platform. The rest were interrogated, and confessed. Then they came to me, and my father immediately appeared with my boy, and withdrew me from the step, and said in a supplicating tone, 'Have pity on your babe.' And Hilarianus the procurator, who had just received the power of life and death in the place of the proconsul Minucius Timinianus, who was deceased, said, 'Spare the grey hairs of your father, spare the infancy of your boy, offer sacrifice for the well-being of the emperors.' And I replied, 'I will not do so.' Hilarianus said, 'Are you a Christian?' And I replied, 'I am a Christian.' And as my father stood there to cast me down from the faith, he was ordered by Hilarianus to be thrown down, and was beaten with rods. And my father's misfortune grieved me as if I myself had been beaten, I so grieved for his wretched old age. The procurator then delivers judgment on all of us, and condemns us to the wild beasts, and we went down cheerfully to the dungeon. Then, because my child had been used to receive suck from me, and to stay with me in the prison, I send Pomponius the deacon to my father to ask for the infant, but my father would not give it him. And even as God willed it, the child no long desired the breast, nor did my breast cause me uneasiness, lest I should be tormented by care for my babe and by the pain of my breasts at once.

3. After a few days, while we were all praying, on a sudden, in the middle of our prayer, there came to me a word, and I named Dinocrates; and I was amazed that that name had never come into my mind until then, and I was grieved as I remembered his misfortune. And I felt myself immediately to be worthy, and to be called on to ask on his behalf. And for him I began earnestly to make supplication, and to cry with groaning to the Lord. Without

delay, on that very night, this was shown to me in a vision. I saw Dinocrates going out from a gloomy place, where also there were several others, and he was parched and very thirsty, with a filthy countenance and pallid colour, and the wound on his face which he had when he died. This Dinocrates had been my brother after the flesh, seven years of age who died miserably with disease— his face being so eaten out with cancer, that his death caused repugnance to all men. For him I had made my prayer, and between him and me there was a large interval, so that neither of us could approach to the other. And moreover, in the same place where Dinocrates was, there was a pool full of water, having its brink higher than was the stature of the boy; and Dinocrates raised himself up as if to drink. And I was grieved that, although that pool held water, still, on account of the height to its brink, he could not drink. And I was aroused, and knew that my brother was in suffering. But I trusted that my prayer would bring help to his suffering; and I prayed for him every day until we passed over into the prison of the camp, for we were to fight in the camp-show. Then was the birth-day of Geta Cæsar, and I made my prayer for my brother day and night, groaning and weeping that he might be granted to me.

4. Then, on the day on which we remained in fetters, this was shown to me. I saw that that place which I had formerly observed to be in gloom was now bright; and Dinocrates, with a clean body well clad, was finding refreshment. And where there had been a wound, I saw a scar; and that pool which I had before seen, I saw now with its margin lowered even to the boy's navel. And one drew water from the pool incessantly, and upon its brink was a goblet filled with water; and Dinocrates drew near and began to drink from it, and the goblet did not fail. And when he was satisfied, he went away from the water to play joyously, after the manner of children, and I awoke. Then I understood that he was translated from the place of punishment.

Chapter 3.
Argument. Perpetua is Again Tempted by Her Father. Her Third Vision, Wherein She is Led Away to Struggle Against an Egyptian. She Fights, Conquers, and Receives the Reward

1. Again, after a few days, Pudens, a soldier, an assistant overseer of the prison, who began to regard us in great esteem, perceiving that the great power of God was in us, admitted many brethren to see us, that both we and they might be mutually refreshed. And when the day of the exhibition drew near, my father, worn with suffering, came in to me, and began to tear out his beard, and to throw himself on the earth, and to cast himself down on his face, and to reproach his years, and to utter such words as might move all creation. I grieved for his unhappy old age.

2. "The day before that on which we were to fight, I saw in a vision that Pomponius the deacon came hither to the gate of the prison, and knocked vehemently. I went out to him, and opened the gate for him; and he was clothed in a richly ornamented white robe, and he had on manifold calliculæ. And he said to me, 'Perpetua, we are waiting for you; come!' And he held his hand to me, and we began to go through rough and winding places. Scarcely at length had we arrived breathless at the amphitheatre, when he led me into the middle of the arena, and said to me, 'Do not fear, I am here with you, and I am labouring with you;' and he departed. And I gazed upon an immense assembly in astonishment. And because I knew that I was given to the wild beasts, I marvelled that the wild beasts were not let loose upon me. Then there came forth against me a certain Egyptian, horrible in appearance, with his backers, to fight with me. And there came to me, as my helpers and encouragers, handsome youths; and I was stripped, and became a man. Then my helpers began to rub me with oil, as is the custom for contest; and I beheld that Egyptian on the other hand rolling in the dust. And a certain man came forth, of wondrous height, so that he even over-topped the top of the amphitheatre; and he wore a loose tunic and a purple robe between two bands over the middle of the breast; and he had on calliculæ of varied form, made of gold and silver; and he carried a rod, as if he were a trainer of gladiators, and a green branch upon which were apples of gold. And he called for silence, and said, 'This Egyptian, if he should overcome this woman, shall kill her with the sword; and if she shall conquer him, she shall receive this branch.' Then he departed. And we drew near to one another, and began to deal out blows. He sought to lay hold of my feet, while I struck at his face with my heels; and I was lifted up in the air, and began thus to thrust at him as if spurning the earth. But when I saw that there was some delay I joined my hands so as to twine my fingers with one another; and I took hold upon his head, and he fell on his face, and I trod upon his head. And the people began to shout, and my backers to exult. And I drew near to the trainer and took the branch; and he kissed me, and said to me, 'Daughter, peace be with you:' and I began to go gloriously to the Sanavivarian gate. Then I awoke, and perceived that I was not to fight with beasts, but against the devil. Still I knew that the victory was awaiting me. This, so far, I have completed several days before the exhibition; but what passed at the exhibition itself let who will write."

Chapter 4.

Argument. Saturus, in a Vision, and Perpetua Being Carried by Angels into the Great Light, Behold the Martyrs. Being Brought to the Throne of God, are Received with a Kiss. They Reconcile Optatus the Bishop and Aspasius the Presbyter

1. Moreover, also, the blessed Saturus related this his vision, which he himself committed to writing:— "We had suffered," says he, and we had gone forth from the flesh, and we were beginning to be borne by four angels into the east; and their hands touched us not. And we floated not supine, looking upwards, but as if ascending a gentle slope. And being set free, we at length saw the first boundless light; and I said, 'Perpetua' (for she was at my side), 'this is what the Lord promised to us; we have received the promise.' And while we are borne by those same four angels, there appears to us a vast space which was like a pleasure-garden, having rose-trees and every kind of flower. And the height of the trees was after the measure of a cypress, and their leaves were falling incessantly. Moreover, there in the pleasure-garden four other angels appeared, brighter than the previous ones, who, when they saw us, gave us honour, and said to the rest of the angels, 'Here they are! Here they are!' with admiration. And those four angels who bore us, being greatly afraid, put us down; and we passed over on foot the space of a furlong in a broad path. There we found Jocundus and Saturninus and Artaxius, who having suffered the same persecution were burnt alive; and Quintus, who also himself a martyr had departed in the prison. And we asked of them where the rest were. And the angels said to us, 'Come first, enter and greet your Lord.'

2. And we came near to place, the walls of which were such as if they were built of light; and before the gate of that place stood four angels, who clothed those who entered with white robes. And being clothed, we entered and saw the boundless light, and heard the united voice of some who said without ceasing, 'Holy! Holy! Holy!' And in the midst of that place we saw as it were an old man sitting, having snow-white hair, and with a youthful countenance; and his feet we saw not. And on his right hand and on his left were four-and-twenty elders, and behind them a great many others were standing. We entered with great wonder, and stood before the throne; and the four angels raised us up, and we kissed Him, and He passed His hand over our face. And the rest of the elders said to us, 'Let us stand;' and we stood and made peace. And the elders said to us, 'Go and enjoy.' And I said, 'Perpetua, you have what you wish.' And she said to me, 'Thanks be to God, that joyous as I was in the flesh, I am now more joyous here.'

3. "And we went forth, and saw before the entrance Optatus the bishop at the right hand, and Aspasius the presbyter, a teacher, at the left hand, separate

and sad; and they cast themselves at our feet, and said to us, 'Restore peace between us, because you have gone forth and have left us thus.' And we said to them, 'Are you not our father, and you our presbyter, that you should cast yourselves at our feet?' And we prostrated ourselves, and we embraced them; and Perpetua began to speak with them, and we drew them apart in the pleasure-garden under a rose-tree. And while we were speaking with them, the angels said unto them, 'Let them alone, that they may refresh themselves; and if you have any dissensions between you, forgive one another.' And they drove them away. And they said to Optatus, 'Rebuke your people, because they assemble to you as if returning from the circus, and contending about factious matters.' And then it seemed to us as if they would shut the doors. And in that place we began to recognise many brethren, and moreover martyrs. We were all nourished with an indescribable odour, which satisfied us. Then, I joyously awoke."

Chapter 5.

Argument. Secundulus Dies in the Prison. Felicitas is Pregnant, But with Many Prayers She Brings Forth in the Eighth Month Without Suffering, the Courage of Perpetua and of Saturus Unbroken

1. The above were the more eminent visions of the blessed martyrs Saturus and Perpetua themselves, which they themselves committed to writing. But God called Secundulus, while he has yet in the prison, by an earlier exit from the world, not without favour, so as to give a respite to the beasts. Nevertheless, even if his soul did not acknowledge cause for thankfulness, assuredly his flesh did.

2. But respecting Felicitas (for to her also the Lord's favour approached in the same way), when she had already gone eight months with child (for she had been pregnant when she was apprehended), as the day of the exhibition was drawing near, she was in great grief lest on account of her pregnancy she should be delayed—because pregnant women are not allowed to be publicly punished—and lest she should shed her sacred and guiltless blood among some who had been wicked subsequently. Moreover, also, her fellow martyrs were painfully saddened lest they should leave so excellent a friend, and as it were companion, alone in the path of the same hope. Therefore, joining together their united cry, they poured forth their prayer to the Lord three days before the exhibition. Immediately after their prayer her pains came upon her, and when, with the difficulty natural to an eight months' delivery, in the labour of bringing forth she was sorrowing, some one of the servants of the Cataractarii said to her, "You who are in such suffering now, what will you do when you are thrown to the beasts, which you despised when you refused to sacrifice?" And she replied, "Now it is I that suffer what I suffer; but then

there will be another in me, who will suffer for me, because I also am about to suffer for Him." Thus she brought forth a little girl, which a certain sister brought up as her daughter.

3. Since then the Holy Spirit permitted, and by permitting willed, that the proceedings of that exhibition should be committed to writing, although we are unworthy to complete the description of so great a glory; yet we obey as it were the command of the most blessed Perpetua, nay her sacred trust, and add one more testimony concerning her constancy and her loftiness of mind. While they were treated with more severity by the tribune, because, from the intimations of certain deceitful men, he feared lest they should be withdrawn from the prison by some sort of magic incantations, Perpetua answered to his face, and said, "Why do you not at least permit us to be refreshed, being as we are objectionable to the most noble Cæsar, and having to fight on his birthday? Or is it not your glory if we are brought forward fatter on that occasion?" The tribune shuddered and blushed, and commanded that they should be kept with more humanity, so that permission was given to their brethren and others to go in and be refreshed with them; even the keeper of the prison trusting them now himself.

4. Moreover, on the day before, when in that last meal, which they call the free meal, they were partaking as far as they could, not of a free supper, but of an agape; with the same firmness they were uttering such words as these to the people, denouncing against them the judgment of the Lord, bearing witness to the felicity of their passion, laughing at the curiosity of the people who came together; while Saturus said, "Tomorrow is not enough for you, for you to behold with pleasure that which you hate. Friends today, enemies tomorrow. Yet note our faces diligently, that you may recognise them on that day of judgment." Thus all departed thence astonished, and from these things many believed.

Chapter 6.

Argument. From the Prison They are Led Forth with Joy into the Amphitheatre, Especially Perpetua and Felicitas. All Refuse to Put on Profane Garments. They are Scourged, They are Thrown to the Wild Beasts. Saturus Twice is Unhurt. Perpetua and Felicitas are Thrown Down; They are Called Back to the Sanavivarian Gate. Saturus Wounded by a Leopard, Exhorts the Soldier. They Kiss One Another, and are Slain with the Sword

1. The day of their victory shone forth, and they proceeded from the prison into the amphitheatre, as if to an assembly, joyous and of brilliant countenances; if perchance shrinking, it was with joy, and not with fear.

Perpetua followed with placid look, and with step and gait as a matron of Christ, beloved of God; casting down the luster of her eyes from the gaze of all. Moreover, Felicitas, rejoicing that she had safely brought forth, so that she might fight with the wild beasts; from the blood and from the midwife to the gladiator, to wash after childbirth with a second baptism. And when they were brought to the gate, and were constrained to put on the clothing— the men, that of the priests of Saturn, and the women, that of those who were consecrated to Ceres— that noble-minded woman resisted even to the end with constancy. For she said, "We have come thus far of our own accord, for this reason, that our liberty might not be restrained. For this reason we have yielded our minds, that we might not do any such thing as this: we have agreed on this with you." Injustice acknowledged the justice; the tribune yielded to their being brought as simply as they were. Perpetua sang psalms, already treading under foot the head of the Egyptian; Revocatus, and Saturninus, and Saturus uttered threatenings against the gazing people about this martyrdom. When they came within sight of Hilarianus, by gesture and nod, they began to say to Hilarianus, "You judge us," say they, "but God will judge you." At this the people, exasperated, demanded that they should be tormented with scourges as they passed along the rank of the venatores. And they indeed rejoiced that they should have incurred any one of their Lord's passions.

2. But He who had said, "Ask, and you shall receive," (John 16:24) gave to them when they asked, that death which each one had wished for. For when at any time they had been discoursing among themselves about their wish in respect of their martyrdom, Saturninus indeed had professed that he wished that he might be thrown to all the beasts; doubtless that he might wear a more glorious crown. Therefore in the beginning of the exhibition he and Revocatus made trial of the leopard, and moreover upon the scaffold they were harassed by the bear. Saturus, however, held nothing in greater abomination than a bear; but he imagined that he would be put an end to with one bite of a leopard. Therefore, when a wild boar was supplied, it was the huntsman rather who had supplied that boar who was gored by that same beast, and died the day after the shows. Saturus only was drawn out; and when he had been bound on the floor near to a bear, the bear would not come forth from his den. And so Saturus for the second time is recalled unhurt.

3. Moreover, for the young women the devil prepared a very fierce cow, provided especially for that purpose contrary to custom, rivalling their sex also in that of the beasts. And so, stripped and clothed with nets, they were led forth. The populace shuddered as they saw one young woman of delicate frame, and another with breasts still dropping from her recent childbirth. So,

being recalled, they are unbound. Perpetua is first led in. She was tossed, and fell on her loins; and when she saw her tunic torn from her side, she drew it over her as a veil for her middle, rather mindful of her modesty than her suffering. Then she was called for again, and bound up her dishevelled hair; for it was not becoming for a martyr to suffer with dishevelled hair, lest she should appear to be mourning in her glory. So she rose up; and when she saw Felicitas crushed, she approached and gave her her hand, and lifted her up. And both of them stood together; and the brutality of the populace being appeased, they were recalled to the Sanavivarian gate. Then Perpetua was received by a certain one who was still a catechumen, Rusticus by name, who kept close to her; and she, as if aroused from sleep, so deeply had she been in the Spirit and in an ecstasy, began to look round her, and to say to the amazement of all, "I cannot tell when we are to be led out to that cow." And when she had heard what had already happened, she did not believe it until she had perceived certain signs of injury in her body and in her dress, and had recognised the catechumen. Afterwards causing that catechumen and the brother to approach, she addressed them, saying, "Stand fast in the faith, and love one another, all of you, and be not offended at my sufferings."

4. The same Saturus at the other entrance exhorted the soldier Pudens, saying, "Assuredly here I am, as I have promised and foretold, for up to this moment I have felt no beast. And now believe with your whole heart. Lo, I am going forth to that beast, and I shall be destroyed with one bite of the leopard." And immediately at the conclusion of the exhibition he was thrown to the leopard; and with one bite of his he was bathed with such a quantity of blood, that the people shouted out to him as he was returning, the testimony of his second baptism, "Saved and washed, saved and washed." Manifestly he was assuredly saved who had been glorified in such a spectacle. Then to the soldier Pudens he said, "Farewell, and be mindful of my faith; and let not these things disturb, but confirm you." And at the same time he asked for a little ring from his finger, and returned it to him bathed in his wound, leaving to him an inherited token and the memory of his blood. And then lifeless he is cast down with the rest, to be slaughtered in the usual place. And when the populace called for them into the midst, that as the sword penetrated into their body they might make their eyes partners in the murder, they rose up of their own accord, and transferred themselves whither the people wished; but they first kissed one another, that they might consummate their martyrdom with the kiss of peace. The rest indeed, immoveable and in silence, received the sword-thrust; much more Saturus, who also had first ascended the ladder, and first gave up his spirit, for he also was waiting for Perpetua. But Perpetua, that she might taste some pain, being pierced between the ribs, cried out loudly, and she herself placed the wavering right hand of the youthful

gladiator to her throat. Possibly such a woman could not have been slain unless she herself had willed it, because she was feared by the impure spirit.

O most brave and blessed martyrs! O truly called and chosen unto the glory of our Lord Jesus Christ! Whom whoever magnifies, and honours, and adores, assuredly ought to read these examples for the edification of the Church, not less than the ancient ones, so that new virtues also may testify that one and the same Holy Spirit is always operating even until now, and God the Father Omnipotent, and His Son Jesus Christ our Lord, whose is the glory and infinite power for ever and ever. Amen.

On the Martyrs
Tertullian of Carthage

Chapter 1

Blessed Martyrs Designate,— Along with the provision which our lady mother the Church from her bountiful breasts, and each brother out of his private means, makes for your bodily wants in the prison, accept also from me some contribution to your spiritual sustenance; for it is not good that the flesh be feasted and the spirit starve: nay, if that which is weak be carefully looked to, it is but right that that which is still weaker should not be neglected. Not that I am specially entitled to exhort you; yet not only the trainers and overseers, but even the unskilled, nay, all who choose, without the slightest need for it, are wont to animate from afar by their cries the most accomplished gladiators, and from the mere throng of onlookers useful suggestions have sometimes come; first, then, O blessed, grieve not the Holy Spirit, who has entered the prison with you; for if He had not gone with you there, you would not have been there this day. Do you give all endeavour, therefore, to retain Him; so let Him lead you thence to your Lord. The prison, indeed, is the devil's house as well, wherein he keeps his family. But you have come within its walls for the very purpose of trampling the wicked one under foot in his chosen abode. You had already in pitched battle outside utterly overcome him; let him have no reason, then, to say to himself, "They are now in my domain; with vile hatreds I shall tempt them, with defections or dissensions among themselves." Let him fly from your presence, and skulk away into his own abysses, shrunken and torpid, as though he were an outcharmed or smoked-out snake. Give him not the success in his own kingdom of setting you at variance with each other, but let him find you armed and fortified with concord; for peace among you is battle with him. Some, not able to find this peace in the Church, have been used to seek it from the imprisoned martyrs. And so you ought to have it dwelling with you, and to cherish it, and to guard it, that you may be able perhaps to bestow it upon others.

Chapter 2

Other things, hindrances equally of the soul, may have accompanied you as far as the prison gate, to which also your relatives may have attended you. There and thenceforth you were severed from the world; how much more from the ordinary course of worldly life and all its affairs! Nor let this separation from the world alarm you; for if we reflect that the world is more really the prison, we shall see that you have gone out of a prison rather than into one. The world has the greater darkness, blinding men's hearts. The world imposes the more grievous fetters, binding men's very souls. The world breathes out the worst impurities— human lusts. The world contains the larger number of criminals, even the whole human race. Then, last of all, it awaits the judgment, not of the proconsul, but of God. Wherefore, O blessed, you may regard yourselves as having been translated from a prison to, we may say, a place of safety. It is full of darkness, but you yourselves are light; it has bonds, but God has made you free. Unpleasant exhalations are there, but you are an odour of sweetness. The judge is daily looked for, but you shall judge the judges themselves. Sadness may be there for him who sighs for the world's enjoyments. The Christian outside the prison has renounced the world, but in the prison he has renounced a prison too. It is of no consequence where you are in the world— you who are not of it. And if you have lost some of life's sweets, it is the way of business to suffer present loss, that after gains may be the larger. Thus far I say nothing of the rewards to which God invites the martyrs. Meanwhile let us compare the life of the world and of the prison, and see if the spirit does not gain more in the prison than the flesh loses. Nay, by the care of the Church and the love of the brethren, even the flesh does not lose there what is for its good, while the spirit obtains besides important advantages. You have no occasion to look on strange gods, you do not run against their images; you have no part in heathen holidays, even by mere bodily mingling in them; you are not annoyed by the foul fumes of idolatrous solemnities; you are not pained by the noise of the public shows, nor by the atrocity or madness or immodesty of their celebrants; your eyes do not fall on stews and brothels; you are free from causes of offense, from temptations, from unholy reminiscences; you are free now from persecution too. The prison does the same service for the Christian which the desert did for the prophet. Our Lord Himself spent much of His time in seclusion, that He might have greater liberty to pray, that He might be quit of the world. It was in a mountain solitude, too, He showed His glory to the disciples. Let us drop the name of prison; let us call it a place of retirement. Though the body is shut in, though the flesh is confined, all things are open to the spirit. In spirit, then, roam abroad; in spirit walk about, not setting before you shady paths or long colonnades, but the way which leads to God. As often as in spirit your footsteps are there, so often you will not be in bonds. The leg does not feel the chain when the mind is in the heavens. The mind compasses the whole man about, and whither it wills it carries him. But where your heart shall be, there shall be your treasure. (Matthew 6:21) Be there our heart, then, where we would have our treasure.

Chapter 3

Grant now, O blessed, that even to Christians the prison is unpleasant; yet we were called to the warfare of the living God in our very response to the sacramental words. Well, no soldier comes out to the campaign laden with luxuries, nor does he go to action from his comfortable chamber, but from the light and narrow tent, where every kind of hardness, roughness and unpleasantness must be put up with. Even in peace soldiers inure themselves to war by toils and inconveniences— marching in arms, running over the plain, working at the ditch, making the testudo, engaging in many arduous labours. The sweat of the brow is on everything, that bodies and minds may not shrink at having to pass from shade to sunshine, from sunshine to icy cold, from the robe of peace to the coat of mail, from silence to clamour, from quiet to tumult. In like manner, O blessed ones, count whatever is hard in this lot of yours as a discipline of your powers of mind and body. You are about to pass through a noble struggle, in which the living God acts the part of superintendent, in which the Holy Ghost is your trainer, in which the prize is an eternal crown of angelic essence, citizenship in the heavens, glory everlasting. Therefore your Master, Jesus Christ, who has anointed you with His Spirit, and led you forth to the arena, has seen it good, before the day of conflict, to take you from a condition more pleasant in itself, and has imposed on you a harder treatment, that your strength might be the greater. For the athletes, too, are set apart to a more stringent discipline, that they may have their physical powers built up. They are kept from luxury, from daintier meats, from more pleasant drinks; they are pressed, racked, worn out; the harder their labours in the preparatory training, the stronger is the hope of victory. "And they," says the apostle, "that they may obtain a corruptible crown." (1 Corinthians 9:25) We, with the crown eternal in our eye, look upon the prison as our training-ground, that at the goal of final judgment we may be brought forth well disciplined by many a trial; since virtue is built up by hardships, as by voluptuous indulgence it is overthrown.

Chapter 4

From the saying of our Lord we know that the flesh is weak, the spirit willing. Matthew 26:41 Let us not, withal, take delusive comfort from the Lord's acknowledgment of the weakness of the flesh. For precisely on this account He first declared the spirit willing, that He might show which of the two ought to be subject to the other— that the flesh might yield obedience to the spirit— the weaker to the stronger; the former thus from the latter getting strength. Let the spirit hold convene with the flesh about the common salvation, thinking no longer of the troubles of the prison, but of the wrestle and conflict for which they are the preparation. The flesh, perhaps, will dread the merciless sword, and the lofty cross, and the rage of the wild beasts, and that punishment of the flames, of all most terrible, and all the skill of the executioner in torture. But, on the other side, let the spirit set clearly before both itself and the flesh, how these things, though exceeding painful, have yet been calmly endured by many—and, have even been eagerly desired for the sake of fame and glory; and this not only in the case of men, but of women too, that you, O holy women, may be worthy of your sex. It would take me too long to enumerate one by one the men who at their own self-impulse have put an end to themselves. As to women, there is a famous case at hand: the violated Lucretia, in the presence of her kinsfolk, plunged the knife into herself, that she might have glory for her chastity. Mucius burned his right hand on an altar, that this deed of his might dwell in fame. The philosophers have been outstripped,— for instance Heraclitus, who, smeared with cow dung, burned himself; and Empedocles, who leapt down into the fires of Ætna; and Peregrinus, who not long ago threw himself on the funeral pile. For women even have despised the flames. Dido did so, lest, after the death of a husband very dear to her, she should be compelled to marry again; and so did the wife of Hasdrubal, who, Carthage being on fire, that she might not behold her husband suppliant as Scipio's feet, rushed with her children into the conflagration, in which her native city was destroyed. Regulus, a Roman general, who had been taken prisoner by the Carthaginians, declined to be exchanged for a large number of Carthaginian captives, choosing rather to be given back to the enemy. He was crammed into a sort of chest; and, everywhere pierced by nails driven from the outside, he endured so many crucifixions. Woman has voluntarily sought the wild beasts, and even asps, those serpents worse than bear or bull, which Cleopatra applied to herself, that she might not fall into the hands of her enemy. But the fear of death is not so great as the fear of torture. And so the Athenian courtezan succumbed to the executioner, when, subjected to torture by the tyrant for having taken part in a conspiracy, still making no betrayal of her confederates, she at last bit off her tongue and spat it in the tyrant's face, that he might be convinced of the uselessness of his torments, however long they should be continued. Everybody knows what to this day is the great Lacedæmonian solemnity— the διαμαστύγωσις, or scourging; in which sacred rite the Spartan youths are beaten with scourges before the altar, their parents and kinsmen standing by and exhorting them to stand it bravely out. For it will be always counted more honourable and glorious that the soul rather than the body has given itself to stripes. But if so high a value is put on the earthly glory, won by mental and bodily vigour, that men, for the praise of their fellows, I may say, despise the sword, the fire, the cross, the wild beasts, the torture; these surely are but trifling sufferings to obtain a celestial glory and a divine reward. If the bit of glass is so precious, what must the true pearl be worth? Are we not called on, then, most joyfully to lay out as much for the true as others do for the false?

Chapter 5

I leave out of account now the motive of glory. All these same cruel and painful conflicts, a mere vanity you find among men— in fact, a sort of mental disease— as trampled under foot. How many ease-lovers does the conceit of arms give to the sword? They actually go down to meet the very wild beasts in vain ambition; and they fancy themselves more winsome from the bites and scars of the contest. Some have sold themselves to fires, to run a certain distance in a burning tunic. Others, with most enduring shoulders, have walked about under the hunters' whips. The Lord has given these things a place in the world, O blessed, not without some reason: for what reason, but now to animate us, and on that day to confound us if we have feared to suffer for the truth, that we might be saved, what others out of vanity have eagerly sought for to their ruin?

Chapter 6

Passing, too, from examples of enduring constancy having such an origin as this, let us turn to a simple contemplation of man's estate in its ordinary conditions, that perhaps from things which happen to us whether we will or no, and which we must set our minds to bear, we may get instruction. How often, then, have fires consumed the living! How often have wild beasts torn men in pieces, it may be in their own forests, or it may be in the heart of cities, when they have chanced to escape from their dens! How many have fallen by the robber's sword! How many have suffered at the hands of enemies the death of the cross, after having been tortured first, yes, and treated with every sort of contumely! One may even suffer in the cause of a man what he hesitates to suffer in the cause of God. In reference to this indeed, let the present time bear testimony, when so many persons of rank have met with death in a mere human being's cause, and that though from their birth and dignities and bodily condition and age such a fate seemed most unlikely; either suffering at his hands if they have taken part against him, or from his enemies if they have been his partisans.

On the Veiling of Virgins
Tertullian of Carthage

Chapter 1. Truth Rather to Be Appealed to Than Custom, and Truth Progressive in Its Developments

Having already undergone the trouble peculiar to my opinion, I will show in Latin also that it behooves our virgins to be veiled from the time that they have passed the turning-point of their age: that this observance is exacted by truth, on which no one can impose prescription— no space of times, no influence of persons, no privilege of regions. For these, for the most part, are the sources whence, from some ignorance or simplicity, custom finds its beginning; and then it is successively confirmed into an usage, and thus is maintained in opposition to truth. But our Lord Christ has surnamed Himself Truth, not Custom. If Christ is always, and prior to all, equally truth is a thing sempiternal and ancient. Let those therefore look to themselves, to whom that is new which is intrinsically old. It is not so much novelty as truth which convicts heresies. Whatever savours of opposition to truth, this will be heresy, even (if it be an) ancient custom. On the other hand, if any is ignorant of anything, the ignorance proceeds from his own defect. Moreover, whatever is matter of ignorance ought to have been as carefully inquired into as whatever is matter of acknowledgment received. The rule of faith, indeed, is altogether one, alone immoveable and irreformable; the rule, to wit, of believing in one only God omnipotent, the Creator of the universe, and His Son Jesus Christ, born of the Virgin Mary, crucified under Pontius Pilate, raised again the third day from the dead, received in the heavens, sitting now at the right (hand) of the Father, destined to come to judge quick and dead through the resurrection of the flesh as well (as of the spirit). This law of faith being constant, the other succeeding points of discipline and conversation admit the "novelty" of correction; the grace of God, to wit, operating and advancing even to the end. For what kind of (supposition) is it, that, while the devil is always operating and adding daily to the ingenuities of iniquity, the work of God should either have ceased, or else have desisted from advancing? Whereas the reason why the Lord sent the Paraclete was, that, since human mediocrity was unable to take in all things at once, discipline should, little by little, be directed, and ordained, and carried on to perfection, by that Vicar of the Lord, the Holy Spirit. "Still," He said, "I have many things to say to you, but you are not yet able to bear them: when that Spirit of truth shall have come, He will conduct you into all truth, and will report to you the supervening (things)." But above, withal, He made a declaration concerning this His work. What, then, is the Paraclete's administrative office but this: the direction of discipline, the revelation of the Scriptures, the reformation of the intellect, the advancement toward the "better things?" Nothing is without stages of growth: all things await their season. In short, the preacher says, "A time to everything." Look how creation itself advances little by little to fructification. First comes the grain, and from the grain arises the shoot, and from the shoot struggles out the shrub: thereafter boughs and leaves gather strength, and the whole that we call a tree expands: then follows the swelling of the germen, and from the germen bursts the flower, and from the flower the fruit opens: that fruit itself, rude for a while, and unshapely, little by little, keeping the straight course of its development, is trained to the mellowness of its flavour. So, too, righteousness— for the God of righteousness and of creation is the same— was first in a rudimentary state, having a natural fear of God: from that stage it advanced, through the Law and the Prophets, to infancy; from that stage it passed, through the Gospel, to the fervour of youth: now, through the Paraclete, it is settling into maturity. He will be, after Christ, the only one to be called and revered as Master; for He speaks not from Himself, but what is commanded by Christ. He is the only prelate, because He alone succeeds Christ. They who have received Him set truth before custom. They who have heard Him prophesying even to the present time, not of old, bid virgins be wholly covered.

Chapter 2. Before Proceeding Farther, Let the Question of Custom Itself Be Sifted

But I will not, meantime, attribute this usage to Truth. Be it, for a while, custom: that to custom I may likewise oppose custom.

Throughout Greece, and certain of its barbaric provinces, the majority of Churches keep their virgins covered. There are places, too, beneath this (African) sky, where this practice obtains; lest any ascribe the custom to Greek or barbarian Gentilehood. But I have proposed (as models) those Churches which were founded by apostles or apostolic men; and antecedently, I think, to certain (founders, who shall be nameless). Those Churches therefore, as well (as others), have the self-same authority of custom (to appeal to); in opposing phalanx they range "times" and "teachers," more than these later (Churches do). What shall we observe? What shall we choose? We cannot contemptuously reject a custom which we cannot condemn, inasmuch as it is not "strange," since it is not among "strangers" that we find it, but among those, to wit, with whom we share the law of peace and the name of brotherhood. They and we have one faith, one God, the same Christ, the same hope, the same baptismal sacraments; let me say it once for all, we are one Church. Thus, whatever belongs to our brethren is ours: only, the body divides us.

Still, here (as generally happens in all cases of various practice, of doubt, and of uncertainty), examination ought to have been made to see which of two so diverse customs were the more compatible with the discipline of God. And, of course, that ought to have been chosen which keeps virgins veiled, as being known to God alone; who (besides that glory must be sought from God, not from men) ought to blush even at their own privilege. You put a virgin to the blush more by praising than by blaming her; because the front of sin is more hard, learning shamelessness from and in the sin itself. For that custom which belies virgins while it exhibits them, would never have been approved by any except by some men who must have been similar in character to the virgins themselves. Such eyes will wish that a virgin be seen as has the virgin who shall wish to be seen. The same kinds of eyes reciprocally crave after each other. Seeing and being seen belong to the self-same lust. To blush if he see a virgin is as much a mark of a chaste man, as of a chaste virgin if seen by a man.

Chapter 3. Gradual Development of Custom, and Its Results. Passionate Appeal to Truth

But not even between customs have those most chaste teachers chosen to examine. Still, until very recently, among us, either custom was, with comparative indifference, admitted to communion. The matter had been left to choice, for each virgin to veil herself or expose herself, as she might have chosen, just as (she had equal liberty) as to marrying, which itself withal is neither enforced nor prohibited. Truth had been content to make an agreement with custom, in order that under the name of custom it might enjoy itself even partially. But when the power of discerning began to advance, so that the licence granted to either fashion was becoming the mean whereby the indication of the better part emerged; immediately the great adversary of good things— and much more of good institutions— set to his own work. The virgins of men go about, in opposition to the virgins of God, with front quite bare, excited to a rash audacity; and the semblance of virgins is exhibited by women who have the power of asking somewhat from husbands, not to say such a request as that (forsooth) their rivals— all the more "free" in that they are the "hand-maids" of Christ alone — may be surrendered to them. "We are scandalized," they say, "because others walk otherwise (than we do);" and they prefer being "scandalized" to being provoked (to modesty). A "scandal," if I mistake not, is an example not of a good thing, but of a bad, tending to sinful edification. Good things scandalize none but an evil mind. If modesty, if bashfulness, if contempt of glory, anxious to please God alone, are good things, let women who are "scandalized" by such good learn to acknowledge their own evil. For what if the incontinent withal say they are "scandalized" by the continent? Is continence to be recalled? And, for fear the multinubists be "scandalized," is monogamy to be rejected? Why may not these latter rather complain that the petulance, the impudence, of ostentatious virginity is a "scandal" to them? Are therefore chaste virgins to be, for the sake of these marketable creatures, dragged into the church, blushing at being recognised in public, quaking at being unveiled, as if they had been invited as it were to rape? For they are no less unwilling to suffer even this. Every public exposure of an honourable virgin is (to her) a suffering of rape: and yet the suffering of carnal violence is the less (evil), because it comes of natural office. But when the very spirit itself is violated in a virgin by the abstraction of her covering, she has learned to lose what she used to keep. O sacrilegious hands, which have had the hardihood to drag off a dress dedicated to God! What worse could any persecutor have done, if he had known that this (garb) had been chosen by a virgin? You have denuded a maiden in regard of her head, and immediately she wholly ceases to be a virgin to herself; she has undergone a change! Arise, therefore, Truth; arise, and as it were burst forth from Your patience! No custom do I wish You to defend; for by this time even that custom under which You enjoyed your own liberty is being stormed! Demonstrate that it is Yourself who art the coverer of virgins. Interpret in person Your own Scriptures, which Custom understands not; for, if she had, she never would have had an existence.

Chapter 4. Of the Argument Drawn from 1 Cor. XI. 5-16.

But in so far as it is the custom to argue even from the Scriptures in opposition to truth, there is immediately urged against us the fact that "no mention of virgins is made by the apostle where he is prescribing about the veil, but that 'women' only are named; whereas, if he had willed virgins as well to be covered, he would have pronounced concerning 'virgins' also together with the 'women' named; just as," says (our opponent), "in that passage where he is treating of marriage, he declares likewise with regard to 'virgins' what observance is to be followed." And accordingly (it is urged) that "they are not comprised in the law of veiling the head, as not being named in this law; nay rather, that this is the origin of their being unveiled, inasmuch as they who are not named are not bidden."

But we withal retort the self-same line of argument. For he who knew elsewhere how to make mention of each sex— of virgin I mean, and woman, that is, not-virgin— for distinction's sake; in these (passages), in which he does not name a virgin, points out (by not making the distinction) community of condition. Otherwise he could here also have marked the difference between virgin and woman, just as elsewhere he says, "Divided is the woman and the virgin." Therefore those whom, by passing them over in silence, he has not divided, he has included in the other species.

Nor yet, because in that case "divided is both woman and virgin," will this division exert its patronizing influence in the present case as well, as some will have it. For how many sayings, uttered on another occasion, have no weight— in cases, to wit, where they are not uttered— unless the subject-matter be the same as on the other occasion, so that the one utterance may suffice! But the former case of virgin and woman is widely "divided" from the present question. "Divided," he says, "is the woman and the virgin." Why? Inasmuch as "the unmarried," that is, the virgin, "is anxious about those (things) which are the Lord's, that she may be holy both in body and in spirit; but the married," that is, the not-virgin, "is anxious how she may please her husband." This will be the interpretation of that "division," having no place in this passage (now under consideration); in which pronouncement is made neither about marriage, nor about the mind and the thought of woman and of virgin, but about the veiling of the head. Of which (veiling) the Holy Spirit, willing that there should be no distinction, willed that by the one name of woman should likewise be understood the virgin; whom, by not specially naming, He has not separated from the woman, and, by not separating, has conjoined to her from whom He has not separated her.

Is it now, then, a "novelty" to use the primary word, and nevertheless to have the other (subordinate divisions) understood in that word, in cases where there is no necessity for individually distinguishing the (various parts of the) universal whole? Naturally, a compendious style of speech is both pleasing and necessary; inasmuch as diffuse speech is both tiresome and vain. So, too, we are content with general words, which comprehend in themselves the understanding of the specialties. Proceed we, then, to the word itself. The word (expressing the) natural (distinction) is female. Of the natural word, the general word is woman. Of the general, again, the special is virgin, or wife, or widow, or whatever other names, even of the successive stages of life, are added hereto. Subject, therefore, the special is to the general (because the general is prior); and the succedent to the antecedent, and the partial to the universal: (each) is implied in the word itself to which it is subject; and is signified in it, because contained in it. Thus neither hand, nor foot, nor any one of the members, requires to be signified when the body is named. And if you say the universe, therein will be both the heaven and the things that are in it—sun and moon, and constellations and stars—and the earth and the seas, and everything that goes to make up the list of elements. You will have named all, when you have named that which is made up of all. So, too, by naming woman, he has named whatever is woman's.

Chapter 5. Of the Word Woman, Especially in Connection with Its Application to Eve

But since they use the name of woman in such a way as to think it inapplicable save to her alone who has known a man, the pertinence of the propriety of this word to the sex itself, not to a grade of the sex, must be proved by us; that virgins as well (as others) may be commonly comprised in it.

When this kind of second human being was made by God for man's assistance, that female was immediately named woman; still happy, still worthy of paradise, still virgin. "She shall be called," said (Adam), "Woman." And accordingly you have the name—I say, not already common to a virgin, but— proper (to her; a name) which from the beginning was allotted to a virgin. But some ingeniously will have it that it was said of the future, "She shall be called woman," as if she were destined to be so when she had resigned her virginity; since he added withal: "For this cause shall a man leave father and mother, and be conglutinated to his own woman; and the two shall be one flesh." Let them therefore among whom that subtlety obtains show us first, if she were surnamed woman with a future reference, what name she meantime received. For without a name expressive of her present quality she cannot have been. But what kind of (hypothesis) is it that one who, with an eye to the future, was called by a definite name, at the present time should have nothing for a surname? On all animals Adam imposed names; and on none on the ground of future condition, but on the ground of the present purpose which each particular nature served; called (as each nature was) by that to which from the beginning it showed a propensity. What, then, was she at that time called? Why, as often as she is named in the Scripture, she has the appellation woman before she was wedded, and never virgin while she was a virgin.

This name was at that time the only one she had, and (that) when nothing was (as yet) said prophetically. For when the Scripture records that "the two were naked, Adam and his woman," neither does this savour of the future, as if it said "his woman" as a presage of " wife;" but because his woman was withal unwedded, as being (formed) from his own substance. "This bone," he says, "out of my bones, and flesh out of my flesh, shall be called woman." Hence, then, it is from the tacit consciousness of nature that the actual divinity of the soul has educed into the ordinary usage of common speech, unawares to men, (just as it has thus educed many other things too which we shall elsewhere be able to show to derive from the Scriptures the origin of their doing and saying,) our fashion of calling our wives our women, however improperly withal we may in some instances speak. For the Greeks, too, who use the name of woman more (than we do) in the sense of wife, have other names appropriate to wife. But I prefer to assign this usage as a testimony to Scripture. For when two are made into one flesh through the marriage-tie, the "flesh of flesh and bone of bones" is called the woman of him of whose substance she begins to be accounted by being made his wife. Thus woman is not by nature a name of wife, but wife by condition is a name of woman. In fine, womanhood is predicable apart from wifehood; but wifehood apart from womanhood is not, because it cannot even exist. Having therefore settled the name of the newly-made female— which (name) is woman— and having explained what she formerly was, that is, having sealed the name to her, he immediately turned to the prophetic reason, so as to say, "On this account shall a man leave father and mother." The name is so truly separate from the prophecy, as far as (the prophecy) from the individual person herself, that of course it is not with reference to Eve herself that (Adam) has uttered (the prophecy), but with a view to those future females whom he has named in the maternal fount of the feminine race. Besides, Adam was not to leave "father and mother"— whom he had not— for the sake of Eve. Therefore that which was prophetically said does not apply to Eve, because it does not to Adam either. For it was predicted with regard to the condition of husbands, who were destined to leave their parents for a woman's sake; which could not chance to Eve, because it could not to Adam either.

If the case is so, it is apparent that she was not surnamed woman on account of a future (circumstance), to whom (that) future (circumstance) did not apply.

To this is added, that (Adam) himself published the reason of the name. For, after saying, "She shall be called woman," he said, "inasmuch as she has been taken out of man"— the man himself withal being still a virgin. But we will speak, too, about the name of man in its own place. Accordingly, let none interpret with a prophetic reference a name which was deduced from another signification; especially since it is apparent when she did receive a name founded upon a future (circumstance)— there, namely, where she is surnamed "Eve," with a personal name now, because the natural one had gone before. For if "Eve" means "the mother of the living," behold, she is surnamed from a future (circumstance)! Behold, she is pre-announced to be a wife, and not a virgin! This will be the name of one who is about to wed; for of the bride (comes) the mother.

Thus in this case too it is shown, that it was not from a future (circumstance) that she was at that time named woman, who was shortly after to receive the name which would be proper to her future condition.

Sufficient answer has been made to this part (of the question).

Chapter 6. The Parallel Case of Mary Considered

Let us now see whether the apostle withal observes the norm of this name in accordance with Genesis, attributing it to the sex; calling the virgin Mary a woman, just as Genesis (does) Eve. For, writing to the Galatians, "God," he says, "sent His own Son, made of a woman," who, of course, is admitted to have been a virgin, albeit Hebion resist (that doctrine). I recognise, too, the angel Gabriel as having been sent to "a virgin." But when he is blessing her, it is "among women," not among virgins, that he ranks her: "Blessed (are) you among women." The angel withal knew that even a virgin is called a woman.

But to these two (arguments), again, there is one who appears to himself to have made an ingenious answer; (to the effect that) inasmuch as Mary was "betrothed," therefore it is that both by angel and apostle she is pronounced a woman; for a "betrothed" is in some sense a "bride." Still, between "in some sense" and "truth" there is difference enough, at all events in the present place: for elsewhere, we grant, we must thus hold. Now, however, it is not as being already wedded that they have pronounced Mary a woman, but as being none the less a female even if she had not been espoused; as having been called by this (name) from the beginning: for that must necessarily have a prejudicating force from which the normal type has descended. Else, as far as relates to the present passage, if Mary is here put on a level with a "betrothed," so that she is called a woman not on the ground of being a female, but on the ground of being assigned to a husband, it immediately follows that Christ was not born of a virgin, because (born) of one "betrothed," who by this fact will have ceased to be a virgin. Whereas, if He was born of a virgin— albeit withal "betrothed," yet intact— acknowledge that even a virgin, even an intact one, is called a woman. Here, at all events, there can be no semblance of speaking prophetically, as if the apostle should have named a future woman, that is, bride, in saying "made of a woman." For he could not be naming a posterior woman, from whom Christ had not to be born— that is, one who had known a man; but she who was then present, who was a virgin, was withal called a woman in consequence of the propriety of this name—vindicated, in accordance with the primordial norm, (as belonging) to a virgin, and thus to the universal class of women.

Chapter 7. Of the Reasons Assigned by the Apostle for Bidding Women to Be Veiled

Turn we next to the examination of the reasons themselves which lead the apostle to teach that the female ought to be veiled, (to see) whether the self-same (reasons) apply to virgins likewise; so that hence also the community of the name between virgins and not-virgins may be established, while the self-same causes which necessitate the veil are found to exist in each case.

If "the man is head of the woman," of course (he is) of the virgin too, from whom comes the woman who has married; unless the virgin is a third generic class, some monstrosity with a head of its own. If "it is shameful for a woman to be shaven or shorn," of course it is so for a virgin. (Hence let the world, the rival of God, see to it, if it asserts that close-cut hair is graceful to a virgin in like manner as that flowing hair is to a boy.) To her, then, to whom it is equally unbecoming to be shaven or shorn, it is equally becoming to be covered. If "the woman is the glory of the man," how much more the virgin, who is a glory withal to herself! If "the woman is of the man," and "for the sake of the man," that rib of Adam was first a virgin. If "the woman ought to have power upon the head," all the more justly ought the virgin, to whom pertains the essence of the cause (assigned for this assertion). For if (it is) on account of the angels— those, to wit, whom we read of as having fallen from God and heaven on account of concupiscence after females— who can presume that it was bodies already defiled, and relics of human lust, which such angels yearned after, so as not rather to have been inflamed for virgins, whose bloom pleads an excuse for human lust likewise? For thus does Scripture withal suggest: "And it came to pass," it says, "when men had begun to grow more numerous upon the earth, there were withal daughters born them; but the sons of God, having descried the daughters of men, that they were fair, took to themselves wives of all whom they elected." For here the Greek name of women does seem to have the sense " wives," inasmuch as mention is made of marriage. When, then, it says "the daughters of men," it manifestly purports virgins, who would be still reckoned as belonging to their parents— for wedded women are called their husbands'— whereas it could have said "the wives of men:" in like manner not naming the angels adulterers, but husbands, while they take unwedded "daughters of men," who it has above said were "born," thus also signifying their virginity: first, "born;" but here, wedded to angels. Anything else I know not that they were except "born" and subsequently wedded. So perilous a face, then, ought to be shaded, which has cast stumbling-stones even so far as heaven: that, when standing in the presence of God, at whose bar it stands accused of the driving of the angels from their (native) confines, it may blush before the other angels as well; and may repress that former evil liberty of its head—(a liberty) now to be exhibited not even before human eyes. But even if they were females already contaminated whom those angels had desired, so much the more "on account of the angels" would it have been the duty of virgins to be veiled, as it would have been the more possible for virgins to have been the cause of the angels' sinning. If, moreover, the apostle further adds the prejudgment of "nature," that redundancy of locks is an honour to a woman, because hair serves for a covering, of course it is most of all to a virgin that this is a distinction; for their very adornment properly consists in this, that, by being massed together upon the crown, it wholly covers the very citadel of the head with an encirclement of hair.

Chapter 8. The Argument E Contrario

The contraries, at all events, of all these (considerations) effect that a man is not to cover his head: to wit, because he has not by nature been gifted with excess of hair; because to be shaven or shorn is not shameful to him; because it was not on his account that the angels transgressed; because his Head is Christ. Accordingly, since the apostle is treating of man and woman— why the latter ought to be veiled, but the former not— it is apparent why he has been silent as to the virgin; allowing, to wit, the virgin to be understood in the woman by the self-same reason by which he forbore to name the boy as implied in the man; embracing the whole order of either sex in the names proper (to each) of woman and man. So likewise Adam, while still intact, is surnamed in Genesis man: "She shall be called," says he, " woman, because she has been taken from her own man." Thus was Adam a man before nuptial intercourse, in like manner as Eve a woman. On either side the apostle has made his sentence apply with sufficient plainness to the universal species of each sex; and briefly and fully, with so well-appointed a definition, he says, " Every woman." What is "every," but of every class, of every order, of every condition, of every dignity, of every age?— if, (as is the case), "every" means total and entire, and in none of its parts defective. But the virgin is withal a part of the woman. Equally, too, with regard to not veiling the man, he says "every." Behold two diverse names, Man and woman— "every one" in each case: two laws, mutually distinctive; on the one hand (a law) of veiling, on the other (a law) of baring. Therefore, if the fact that it is said "every man" makes it plain that the name of man is common even to him who is not yet a man, a stripling male; (if), moreover, since the name is common according to nature, the law of not veiling him who among men is a virgin is common too according to discipline: why is it that it is not consequently prejudged that, woman being named, every woman- virgin is similarly comprised in the fellowship of the name, so as to be comprised too in the community of the law? If a virgin is not a woman, neither is a stripling a man. If the virgin is not covered on the plea that she is not a woman, let the stripling be covered on the plea that he is not a man. Let identity of virginity share equality of indulgence. As virgins are not compelled to be veiled, so let boys not be bidden to be unveiled. Why do we partly acknowledge the definition of the apostle, as absolute with regard to "every man," without entering upon disquisitions as to why he has not withal named the boy; but partly prevaricate, though it is equally absolute with regard to "every woman?" "If any," he says, "is contentious, we have not such a custom, nor (has) the Church of God." He shows that there had been some contention about this point; for the extinction whereof he uses the whole compendiousness (of language): not naming the virgin, on the one hand, in order to show that there is to be no doubt about her veiling; and, on the other hand, naming "every woman," whereas he would have named the virgin (had the question been confined to her). So, too, did the Corinthians themselves understand him. In fact, at this day the Corinthians do veil their virgins. What the apostles taught, their disciples approve.

Chapter 9. Veiling Consistent with the Other Rules of Discipline Observed by Virgins and Women in General

Let us now see whether, as we have shown the arguments drawn from nature and the matter itself to be applicable to the virgin as well (as to other females), so likewise the precepts of ecclesiastical discipline concerning women have an eye to the virgin.

It is not permitted to a woman to speak in the church; but neither (is it permitted her) to teach, nor to baptize, nor to offer, nor to claim to herself a lot in any manly function, not to say (in any) sacerdotal office. Let us inquire whether any of these be lawful to a virgin. If it is not lawful to a virgin, but she is subjected on the self-same terms (as the woman), and the necessity for humility is assigned her together with the woman, whence will this one thing be lawful to her which is not lawful to any and every female? If any is a virgin, and has proposed to sanctify her flesh, what prerogative does she (thereby) earn adverse to her own condition? Is the reason why it is granted her to dispense with the veil, that she may be notable and marked as she enters the church? That she may display the honour of sanctity in the liberty of her head? More worthy distinction could have been conferred on her by according her some prerogative of manly rank or office! I know plainly, that in a certain place a virgin of less than twenty years of age has been placed in the order of widows! Whereas if the bishop had been bound to accord her any relief, he might, of course, have done it in some other way without detriment to the respect due to discipline; that such a miracle, not to say monster, should not be pointed at in the church, a virgin-widow! the more portentous indeed, that not even as a widow did she veil her head; denying herself either way; both as virgin, in that she is counted a widow, and as widow, in that she is styled a virgin. But the authority which licenses her sitting in that seat uncovered is the same which allows her to sit there as a virgin: a seat to which (besides the "sixty years" not merely "single-husbanded" (women)— that is, married women— are at length elected, but "mothers" to boot, yes, and "educators of children;" in order, forsooth, that their experimental training in all the affections may, on the one hand, have rendered them capable of readily aiding all others with counsel and comfort, and that, on the other, they may none the less have travelled down the whole course of probation whereby a female can be tested. So true is it, that, on the ground of her position, nothing in the way of public honour is permitted to a virgin.

Chapter 10. If the Female Virgins are to Be Thus Conspicuous, Why Not the Male as Well?

Nor, similarly, (is it permitted) on the ground of any distinctions whatever. Otherwise, it were sufficiently discourteous, that while females, subjected as they are throughout to men, bear in their front an honourable mark of their virginity, whereby they may be looked up to and gazed at on all sides and magnified by the brethren, so many men-virgins, so many voluntary eunuchs, should carry their glory in secret, carrying no token to make them, too, illustrious. For they, too, will be bound to claim some distinctions for themselves— either the feathers of the Garamantes, or else the fillets of the barbarians, or else the cicadas of the Athenians, or else the curls of the Germans, or else the tattoo-marks of the Britons; or else let the opposite course be taken, and let them lurk in the churches with head veiled. Sure we are that the Holy Spirit could rather have made some such concession to males, if He had made it to females; forasmuch as, besides the authority of sex, it would have been more becoming that males should have been honoured on the ground of continency itself likewise. The more their sex is eager and warm toward females, so much the more toil does the continence of (this) greater ardour involve; and therefore the worthier is it of all ostentation, if ostentation of virginity is dignity. For is not continence withal superior to virginity, whether it be the continence of the widowed, or of those who, by consent, have already renounced the common disgrace (which matrimony involves)? For constancy of virginity is maintained by grace; of continence, by virtue. For great is the struggle to overcome concupiscence when you have become accustomed to such concupiscence; whereas a concupiscence the enjoyment whereof you have never known you will subdue easily, not having an adversary (in the shape of) the concupiscence of enjoyment. How, then, would God have failed to make any such concession to men more (than to women), whether on the ground of nearer intimacy, as being "His own image," or on the ground of harder toil? But if nothing (has been thus conceded) to the male, much more to the female.

Chapter 11. The Rule of Veiling Not Applicable to Children

But what we intermitted above for the sake of the subsequent discussion— not to dissipate its coherence— we will now discharge by an answer. For when we joined issue about the apostle's absolute definition, that " every woman" must be understood (as meaning woman) of even every age, it might be replied by the opposite side, that in that case it behooved the virgin to be veiled from her nativity, and from the first entry of her age (upon the roll of time).

But it is not so; but from the time when she begins to be self-conscious, and to awake to the sense of her own nature, and to emerge from the virgin's (sense), and to experience that novel (sensation) which belongs to the succeeding age. For withal the founders of the race, Adam and Eve, so long as they were without intelligence, went "naked;" but after they tasted of "the tree of recognition," they were first sensible of nothing more than of their cause for shame. Thus they each marked their intelligence of their own sex by a covering. But even if it is "on account of the angels" that she is to be veiled, doubtless the age from which the law of the veil will come into operation will be that from which "the daughters of men" were able to invite concupiscence of their persons, and to experience marriage. For a virgin ceases to be a virgin from the time that it becomes possible for her not to be one. And accordingly, among Israel, it is unlawful to deliver one to a husband except after the attestation by blood of her maturity; thus, before this indication, the nature is unripe. Therefore if she is a virgin so long as she is unripe, she ceases to be a virgin when she is perceived to be ripe; and, as not-virgin, is now subject to the law, just as she is to marriage. And the betrothed indeed have the example of Rebecca, who, when she was being conducted— herself still unknown— to an unknown betrothed, as soon as she learned that he whom she had sighted from afar was the man, awaited not the grasp of the hand, nor the meeting of the kiss, nor the interchange of salutation; but confessing what she had felt— namely, that she had been (already) wedded in spirit— denied herself to be a virgin by then and there veiling herself. Oh woman already belonging to Christ's discipline! For she showed that marriage likewise, as fornication is, is transacted by gaze and mind; only that a Rebecca likewise some do still veil. With regard to the rest, however (that is, those who are not betrothed), let the procrastination of their parents, arising from straitened means or scrupulosity, look (to them); let the vow of continence itself look (to them). In no respect does (such procrastination) pertain to an age which is already running its own assigned course, and paying its own dues to maturity. Another secret mother, Nature, and another hidden father, Time, have wedded their daughter to their own laws. Behold that virgin-daughter of yours already wedded— her soul by expectancy, her flesh by transformation— for whom you are preparing a second husband! Already her voice is changed, her limbs fully formed, her "shame" everywhere clothing itself, the months paying their tributes; and do you deny her to be a woman whom you assert to be undergoing womanly experiences? If the contact of a man makes a woman, let there be no covering except after actual experience of marriage. Nay, but even among the heathens (the betrothed) are led veiled to the husband. But if it is at betrothal that they are veiled, because (then) both in body and in spirit they have mingled with a male, through the kiss and the right hands, through which means they first in spirit unsealed their modesty, through the common pledge of conscience whereby they mutually plighted their whole confusion; how much more will time veil them?— (time) without which espoused they cannot be; and by whose urgency, without espousals, they cease to be virgins. Time even the heathens observe, that, in obedience to the law of nature, they may render their own rights to the (different) ages. For their females they dispatch to their businesses from (the age of) twelve years, but the male from two years later; decreeing puberty (to consist) in years, not in espousals or nuptials. "Housewife" one is called, albeit a virgin, and "house-father," albeit a stripling. By us not even natural laws are observed; as if the God of nature were some other than ours!

Chapter 12. Womanhood Self-Evident, and Not to Be Concealed by Just Leaving the Head Bare

Recognise the woman, ay, recognise the wedded woman, by the testimonies both of body and of spirit, which she experiences both in conscience and in flesh. These are the earlier tablets of natural espousals and nuptials. Impose a veil externally upon her who has (already) a covering internally. Let her whose lower parts are not bare have her upper likewise covered. Would you know what is the authority which age carries? Set before yourself each (of these two); one prematurely compressed in woman's garb, and one who, though advanced in maturity, persists in virginity with its appropriate garb: the former will more easily be denied to be a woman than the latter believed a virgin. Such is, then, the honesty of age, that there is no overpowering it even by garb. What of the fact that these (virgins) of ours confess their change of age even by their garb; and, as soon as they have understood themselves to be women, withdraw themselves from virgins, laying aside (beginning with their head itself) their former selves: dye their hair; and fasten their hair with more wanton pin; professing manifest womanhood with their hair parted from the front. The next thing is, they consult the looking-glass to aid their beauty, and thin down their over-exacting face with washing, perhaps withal vamp it up with cosmetics, toss their mantle about them with an air, fit tightly the multiform shoe, carry down more ample appliances to the baths. Why should I pursue particulars? But their manifest appliances alone exhibit their perfect womanhood: yet they wish to play the virgin by the sole fact of leaving their head bare— denying by one single feature what they profess by their entire deportment.

Chapter 13. If Unveiling Be Proper, Why Not Practise It Always, Out of the Church as Well as in It?

If on account of men they adopt a false garb, let them carry out that garb fully even for that end; and as they veil their head in presence of heathens, let them at all events in the church conceal their virginity, which they do veil outside the church. They fear strangers: let them stand in awe of the brethren too; or else let them have the consistent hardihood to appear as virgins in the streets as well, as they have the hardihood to do in the churches. I will praise their vigour, if they succeed in selling anything of virginity among the heathens withal. Identity of nature abroad as at home, identity of custom in the presence of men as of the Lord, consists in identity of liberty. To what purpose, then, do they thrust their glory out of sight abroad, but expose it in the church? I demand a reason. Is it to please the brethren, or God Himself? If God Himself, He is as capable of beholding whatever is done in secret, as He is just to remunerate what is done for His sole honour. In fine, He enjoins us not to trumpet forth any one of those things which will merit reward in His sight, nor get compensation for them from men. But if we are prohibited from letting "our left hand know" when we bestow the gift of a single halfpenny, or any eleemosynary bounty whatever, how deep should be the darkness in which we ought to enshroud ourselves when we are offering God so great an oblation of our very body and our very spirit— when we are consecrating to Him our very nature! It follows, therefore, that what cannot appear to be done for God's sake (because God wills not that it be done in such a way) is done for the sake of men—a thing, of course, primarily unlawful, as betraying a lust of glory. For glory is a thing unlawful to those whose probation consists in humiliation of every kind. And if it is by God that the virtue of continence is conferred, "why do you glory, as if you have not received?" If, however, you have not received it, "what have you which has not been given you?" But by this very fact it is plain that it has not been given you by God— that it is not to God alone that you offer it. Let us see, then, whether what is human be firm and true.

Chapter 14. Perils to the Virgins Themselves Attendant Upon Not-Veiling

They report a saying uttered at one time by some one when first this question was mooted, "And how shall we invite the other (virgins) to similar conduct?" Forsooth, it is their numbers that will make us happy, and not the grace of

God and the merits of each individual! Is it virgins who (adorn or commend) the Church in the sight of God, or the Church which adorns or commends virgins? (Our objector) has therefore confessed that "glory" lies at the root of the matter. Well, where glory is, there is solicitation; where solicitation, there compulsion; where compulsion, there necessity; where necessity, there infirmity. Deservedly, therefore, while they do not cover their head, in order that they may be solicited for the sake of glory, they are forced to cover their bellies by the ruin resulting from infirmity. For it is emulation, not religion, which impels them. Sometimes it is that god— their belly — himself; because the brotherhood readily undertakes the maintenance of virgins. But, moreover, it is not merely that they are ruined, but they draw after them "a long rope of sins." For, after being brought forth into the midst (of the church), and elated by the public appropriation of their property, and laden by the brethren with every honour and charitable bounty, so long as they do not fall,— when any sin has been committed, they meditate a deed as disgraceful as the honour was high which they had. (It is this.) If an uncovered head is a recognised mark of virginity, (then) if any virgin falls from the grace of virginity, she remains permanently with head uncovered for fear of discovery, and walks about in a garb which then indeed is another's. Conscious of a now undoubted womanhood, they have the audacity to draw near to God with head bare. But the "jealous God and Lord," who has said, "Nothing covered which shall not be revealed," brings such in general before the public gaze; for confess they will not, unless betrayed by the cries of their infants themselves. But, in so far as they are "more numerous," will you not just have them suspected of the more crimes? I will say (albeit I would rather not) it is a difficult thing for one to turn woman once for all who fears to do so, and who, when already so turned (in secret), has the power of (still) falsely pretending to be a virgin under the eye of God. What audacities, again, will (such an one) venture on with regard to her womb, for fear of being detected in being a mother as well! God knows how many infants He has helped to perfection and through gestation till they were born sound and whole, after being long fought against by their mothers! Such virgins ever conceive with the readiest facility, and have the happiest deliveries, and children indeed most like to their fathers!

These crimes does a forced and unwilling virginity incur. The very concupiscence of non-concealment is not modest: it experiences somewhat which is no mark of a virgin—the study of pleasing, of course, ay, and (of pleasing) men. Let her strive as much as you please with an honest mind; she must necessarily be imperilled by the public exhibition of herself, while she is penetrated by the gaze of untrustworthy and multitudinous' eyes, while she is tickled by pointing fingers, while she is too well loved, while she feels a warmth creep over her amid assiduous embraces and kisses. Thus the forehead hardens; thus the sense of shame wears away; thus it relaxes; thus is learned the desire of pleasing in another way!

Chapter 15. Of Fascination

Nay, but true and absolute and pure virginity fears nothing more than itself. Even female eyes it shrinks from encountering. Other eyes itself has. It betakes itself for refuge to the veil of the head as to a helmet, as to a shield, to protect its glory against the blows of temptations, against the dam of scandals, against suspicions and whispers and emulation; (against) envy also itself. For there is a something even among the heathens to be apprehended, which they call Fascination, the too unhappy result of excessive praise and glory. This we sometimes interpretatively ascribe to the devil, for of him comes hatred of good; sometimes we attribute it to God, for of Him comes judgment upon haughtiness, exalting, as He does, the humble, and depressing the elated. The more holy virgin, accordingly, will fear, even under the name of fascination, on the one hand the adversary, on the other God, the envious disposition of the former, the censorial light of the latter; and will joy in being known to herself alone and to God. But even if she has been recognized by any other, she is wise to have blocked up the pathway against temptations. For who will have the audacity to intrude with his eyes upon a shrouded face? A face without feeling? A face, so to say, morose? Any evil cogitation whatsoever will be broken by the very severity. She who conceals her virginity, by that fact denies even her womanhood.

Chapter 16. Tertullian, Having Shown His Defence to Be Consistent with Scripture, Nature, and Discipline, Appeals to the Virgins Themselves

Herein consists the defence of our opinion, in accordance with Scripture, in accordance with Nature, in accordance with Discipline. Scripture founds the law; Nature joins to attest it; Discipline exacts it. Which of these (three) does a custom founded on (mere) opinion appear in behalf of? Or what is the colour of the opposite view? God's is Scripture; God's is Nature; God's is Discipline. Whatever is contrary to these is not God's. If Scripture is uncertain, Nature is manifest; and concerning Nature's testimony Scripture cannot be uncertain. If there is a doubt about Nature, Discipline points out what is more sanctioned by God. For nothing is to Him dearer than humility; nothing more acceptable than modesty; nothing more offensive than "glory" and the study of men-pleasing. Let that, accordingly, be to you Scripture, and Nature, and Discipline, which you shall find to have been sanctioned by God; just as you are bidden to "examine all things, and diligently follow whatever is better."

It remains likewise that we turn to (the virgins) themselves, to induce them to accept these (suggestions) the more willingly. I pray you, be you mother, or sister, or virgin-daughter— let me address you according to the names proper to your years— veil your head: if a mother, for your sons' sakes; if a sister, for your brethren's sakes; if a daughter for your fathers' sakes. All ages are perilled in your person. Put on the panoply of modesty; surround yourself with the stockade of bashfulness; rear a rampart for your sex, which must neither allow your own eyes egress nor ingress to other people's. Wear the full garb of woman, to preserve the standing of virgin. Belie somewhat of your inward consciousness, in order to exhibit the truth to God alone. And yet you do not belie yourself in appearing as a bride. For wedded you are to Christ: to Him you have surrendered your flesh; to Him you have espoused your maturity. Walk in accordance with the will of your Espoused. Christ is He who bids the espoused and wives of others veil themselves; (and,) of course, much more His own.

Chapter 17. An Appeal to the Married Women

But we admonish you, too, women of the second (degree of) modesty, who have fallen into wedlock, not to outgrow so far the discipline of the veil, not even in a moment of an hour, as, because you cannot refuse it, to take some other means to nullify it, by going neither covered nor bare. For some, with their turbans and woollen bands, do not veil their head, but bind it up; protected, indeed, in front, but, where the head properly lies, bare. Others are to a certain extent covered over the region of the brain with linen coifs of small dimensions— I suppose for fear of pressing the head— and not reaching quite to the ears. If they are so weak in their hearing as not to be able to hear through a covering, I pity them. Let them know that the whole head constitutes "the woman." Its limits and boundaries reach as far as the place where the robe begins. The region of the veil is co-extensive with the space covered by the hair when unbound; in order that the necks too may be encircled. For it is they which must be subjected, for the sake of which "power" ought to be "had on the head:" the veil is their yoke. Arabia's heathen females will be your judges, who cover not only the head, but the face also, so entirely, that they are content, with one eye free, to enjoy rather half the light than to prostitute the entire face. A female would rather see than be seen. And for this reason a certain Roman queen said that they were most unhappy, in that they could more easily fall in love than be fallen in love with; whereas they are rather happy in their immunity from that second (and indeed more frequent) infelicity, that females are more apt to be fallen in love with than to fall in love. And the modesty of heathen discipline, indeed, is more simple, and, so to say, more barbaric. To us the Lord has, even by revelations, measured the space for the veil to extend over. For a certain sister of ours was thus addressed by an angel, beating her neck, as if in applause: "Elegant neck, and deservedly bare! It is well for you to unveil yourself from the head right down to the loins, lest withal this freedom of your neck profit you not!" And, of course, what you have said to one you have said to all. But how severe a chastisement will they likewise deserve, who, amid (the recital of) the Psalms, and at any mention of (the name of) God, continue uncovered; (who) even when about to spend time in prayer itself, with the utmost readiness place a fringe, or a tuft, or any thread whatever, on the crown of their heads, and suppose themselves to be covered? Of so small extent do they falsely imagine their head to be! Others, who think the palm of their hand plainly greater than any fringe or thread, misuse their head no less; like a certain (creature), more beast than bird, albeit winged, with small head, long legs, and moreover of erect carriage. She, they say, when she has to hide, thrusts away into a thicket her head alone— plainly the whole of it, (though)— leaving all the rest of herself exposed. Thus, while she is secure in head, (but) bare in her larger parts, she is taken wholly, head and all. Such will be their plight withal, covered as they are less than is useful.

It is incumbent, then, at all times and in every place, to walk mindful of the law, prepared and equipped in readiness to meet every mention of God; who, if He be in the heart, will be recognised as well in the head of females. To such as read these (exhortations) with good will, to such as prefer Utility to Custom, may peace and grace from our Lord Jesus Christ redound: as likewise to Septimius Tertullianus, whose this tractate is.

On the Apparel of Women
Tertullian of Carthage

Book I
Chapter 1. Introduction. Modesty in Apparel Becoming to Women, in Memory of the Introduction of Sin into the World Through a Woman

If there dwelt upon earth a faith as great as is the reward of faith which is expected in the heavens, no one of you at all, best beloved sisters, from the time that she had first "known the Lord," and learned (the truth) concerning her own (that is, woman's) condition, would have desired too gladsome (not to say too ostentatious) a style of dress; so as not rather to go about in humble garb, and rather to affect meanness of appearance, walking about as Eve mourning and repentant, in order that by every garb of penitence she might the more fully expiate that which she derives from Eve,— the ignominy, I mean, of the first sin, and the odium (attaching to her as the cause) of human perdition. "In pains and in anxieties do you bear (children), woman; and toward your husband (is) your inclination, and he lords it over you." And do you not know that you are (each) an Eve? The sentence of God on this sex of yours lives in this age: the guilt must of necessity live too. You are the devil's gateway: you are the unsealer of that (forbidden) tree: you are the first deserter of the divine law: you are she who persuaded him whom the devil was not valiant enough to attack. You destroyed so easily God's image, man. On account of your desert— that is, death— even the Son of God had to die. And do you think about adorning yourself over and above your tunics of skins? Come, now; if from the beginning of the world the Milesians sheared sheep, and the Serians spun trees, and the Tyrians dyed, and the Phrygians embroidered with the needle, and the Babylonians with the loom, and pearls gleamed, and onyx-stones flashed; if gold itself also had already issued, with the cupidity (which accompanies it), from the ground; if the mirror, too, already had licence to lie so largely, Eve, expelled from paradise, (Eve) already dead, would also have coveted these things, I imagine! No more, then, ought she now to crave, or be acquainted with (if she desires to live again), what, when she was living, she had neither had nor known. Accordingly these things are all the baggage of woman in her condemned and dead state, instituted as if to swell the pomp of her funeral.

Chapter 2. The Origin of Female Ornamentation, Traced Back to the Angels Who Had Fallen.

For they, withal, who instituted them are assigned, under condemnation, to the penalty of death—those angels, to wit, who rushed from heaven on the daughters of men; so that this ignominy also attaches to woman. For when to an age much more ignorant (than ours) they had disclosed certain well-concealed material substances, and several not well-revealed scientific arts— if it is true that they had laid bare the operations of metallurgy, and had divulged the natural properties of herbs, and had promulgated the powers of enchantments, and had traced out every curious art, even to the interpretation of the stars— they conferred properly and as it were peculiarly upon women that instrumental mean of womanly ostentation, the radiances of jewels wherewith necklaces are variegated, and the circlets of gold wherewith the arms are compressed, and the medicaments of orchil with which wools are coloured, and that black powder itself wherewith the eyelids and eyelashes are made prominent. What is the quality of these things may be declared meantime, even at this point, from the quality and condition of their teachers: in that sinners could never have either shown or supplied anything conducive to integrity, unlawful lovers anything conducive to chastity, renegade spirits anything conducive to the fear of God. If (these things) are to be called teachings, ill masters must of necessity have taught ill; if as wages of lust, there is nothing base of which the wages are honourable. But why was it of so much importance to show these things as well as to confer them? Was it that women, without material causes of splendour, and without ingenious contrivances of grace, could not please men, who, while still unadorned, and uncouth and— so to say— crude and rude, had moved (the mind of) angels? Or was it that the lovers would appear sordid and— through gratuitous use— contumelious, if they had conferred no (compensating) gift on the women who had been enticed into connubial connection with them? But these questions admit of no calculation. Women who possessed angels (as husbands) could desire nothing more; they had, forsooth, made a grand match! Assuredly they who, of course, did sometimes think whence they had fallen, and, after the heated impulses of their lusts, looked up toward heaven, thus requited that very excellence of women, natural beauty, as (having proved) a cause of evil, in order that their good fortune might profit them nothing; but that, being turned from simplicity and sincerity, they, together with (the angels) themselves, might become offensive to God. Sure they were that all ostentation, and ambition, and love of pleasing by carnal means, was displeasing to God. And these are the angels whom we are destined to judge: these are the angels whom in baptism we renounce: these, of course, are the reasons why they have deserved to be judged by man. What business, then, have their things with their judges? What commerce have they who are to condemn with them who are to be condemned? The same, I take it, as Christ has with Belial. With what consistency do we mount that (future) judgment-seat to pronounce sentence against those whose gifts we (now) seek after? For you too, (women as you are,) have the self-same angelic nature promised as your reward, the self-same sex as men: the self-same advancement to the dignity of judging, does (the Lord) promise you. Unless, then, we begin even here to pre-judge, by pre-condemning their things, which we are hereafter to condemn in themselves, they will rather judge and condemn us.

Chapter 3. Concerning the Genuineness of "The Prophecy of Enoch."

I am aware that the Scripture of Enoch, which has assigned this order (of action) to angels, is not received by some, because it is not admitted into the Jewish canon either. I suppose they did not think that, having been published before the deluge, it could have safely survived that world-wide calamity, the abolisher of all things. If that is the reason (for rejecting it), let them recall to their memory that Noah, the survivor of the deluge, was the great-grandson of Enoch himself; and he, of course, had heard and remembered, from domestic renown and hereditary tradition, concerning his own great-grandfather's "grace in the sight of God," and concerning all his preachings; since Enoch had given no other charge to Methuselah than that he should hand on the knowledge of them to his posterity. Noah therefore, no doubt, might have succeeded in the trusteeship of (his) preaching; or, had the case been otherwise, he would not have been silent alike concerning the disposition (of things) made by God, his Preserver, and concerning the particular glory of his own house.

If (Noah) had not had this (conservative power) by so short a route, there would (still) be this (consideration) to warrant our assertion of (the genuineness of) this Scripture: he could equally have renewed it, under the Spirit's inspiration, after it had been destroyed by the violence of the deluge, as, after the destruction of Jerusalem by the Babylonian storming of it, every document of the Jewish literature is generally agreed to have been restored through Ezra.

But since Enoch in the same Scripture has preached likewise concerning the Lord, nothing at all must be rejected by us which pertains to us; and we read that "every Scripture suitable for edification is divinely inspired." By the Jews it may now seem to have been rejected for that (very) reason, just like all the other (portions) nearly which tell of Christ. Nor, of course, is this fact wonderful, that they did not receive some Scriptures which spoke of Him whom even in person, speaking in their presence, they were not to receive. To these considerations is added the fact that Enoch possesses a testimony in the Apostle Jude.

Chapter 4. Waiving the Question of the Authors, Tertullian Proposes to Consider the Things on Their Own Merits

Grant now that no mark of pre-condemnation has been branded on womanly pomp by the (fact of the) fate of its authors; let nothing be imputed to those angels besides their repudiation of heaven and (their) carnal marriage: let us examine the qualities of the things themselves, in order that we may detect the purposes also for which they are eagerly desired.

Female habit carries with it a twofold idea— dress and ornament. By "dress" we mean what they call "womanly gracing;" by "ornament," what it is suitable should be called "womanly disgracing." The former is accounted (to consist) in gold, and silver, and gems, and garments; the latter in care of the hair, and of the skin, and of those parts of the body which attract the eye. Against the one we lay the charge of ambition, against the other of prostitution; so that even from this early stage (of our discussion) you may look forward and see what, out of (all) these, is suitable, handmaid of God, to your discipline, inasmuch as you are assessed on different principles (from other women)— those, namely, of humility and chastity.

Chapter 5. Gold and Silver Not Superior in Origin or in Utility to Other Metals

Gold and silver, the principal material causes of worldly splendour, must necessarily be identical (in nature) with that out of which they have their being: (they must be) earth, that is; (which earth itself is) plainly more glorious (than they), inasmuch as it is only after it has been tearfully wrought by penal labour in the deadly laboratories of accursed mines, and there left its name of "earth" in the fire behind it, that, as a fugitive from the mine, it passes from torments to ornaments, from punishments to embellishments, from ignominies to honours. But iron, and brass, and other the vilest material substances, enjoy a parity of condition (with silver and gold), both as to earthly origin and metallurgic operation; in order that, in the estimation of nature, the substance of gold and of silver may be judged not a whit more noble (than theirs). But if it is from the quality of utility that gold and silver derive their glory, why, iron and brass excel them; whose usefulness is so disposed (by the Creator), that they not only discharge functions of their own more numerous and more necessary to human affairs, but do also none the less serve the turn of gold and silver, by dint of their own powers, in the service of juster causes. For not only are rings made of iron, but the memory of antiquity still preserves (the fame of) certain vessels for eating and drinking made out of brass. Let the insane plenteousness of gold and silver look to it, if it serves to make utensils even for foul purposes. At all events, neither is the field tilled by means of gold, nor the ship fastened together by the strength of silver. No mattock plunges a golden edge into the ground; no nail drives a silver point into planks. I leave unnoticed the fact that the needs of our whole life are dependent upon iron and brass; whereas those rich materials themselves, requiring both to be dug up out of mines, and needing a forging process in every use (to which they are put), are helpless without the laborious vigour of iron and brass. Already, therefore, we must judge whence it is that so high dignity accrues to gold and silver, since they get precedence over material substances which are not only cousin-german to them in point of origin, but more powerful in point of usefulness.

Chapter 6. Of Precious Stones and Pearls

But, in the next place, what am I to interpret those jewels to be which vie with gold in haughtiness, except little pebbles and stones and paltry particles of the self-same earth; but yet not necessary either for laying down foundations, or rearing party-walls, or supporting pediments, or giving density to roofs? The only edifice which they know how to rear is this silly pride of women: because they require slow rubbing that they may shine, and artful underlaying that they may show to advantage, and careful piercing that they may hang; and (because they) render to gold a mutual assistance in meretricious allurement. But whatever it is that ambition fishes up from the British or the Indian sea, it is a kind of conch not more pleasing in savour than— I do not say the oyster and the sea-snail, but— even the giant muscle. For let me add that I know conchs (which are) sweet fruits of the sea. But if that (foreign) conch suffers from some internal pustule, that ought to be regarded rather as its defect than as its glory; and although it be called "pearl," still something else must be understood than some hard, round excrescence of the fish. Some say, too, that gems are culled from the foreheads of dragons, just as in the brains of fishes there is a certain stony substance. This also was wanting to the Christian woman, that she may add a grace to herself from the serpent! Is it thus that she will set her heel on the devil's head, while she heaps ornaments (taken) from his head on her own neck, or on her very head?

Chapter 7. Rarity the Only Cause Which Makes Such Things Valuable

It is only from their rarity and outlandishness that all these things possess their grace; in short, within their own native limits they are not held of so high worth. Abundance is always contumelious toward itself. There are some barbarians with whom, because gold is indigenous and plentiful, it is customary to keep (the criminals) in their convict establishments chained with gold, and to lade the wicked with riches— the more guilty, the more wealthy. At last there has really been found a way to prevent even gold from being loved! We have also seen at Rome the nobility of gems blushing in the presence of our matrons at the contemptuous usage of the Parthians and

Medes, and the rest of their own fellow-countrymen, only that (their gems) are not generally worn with a view to ostentation. Emeralds lurk in their belts; and the sword (that hangs) below their bosom alone is witness to the cylindrical stones that decorate its hilt; and the massive single pearls on their boots are fain to get lifted out of the mud! In short, they carry nothing so richly gemmed as that which ought not to be gemmed if it is (either) not conspicuous, or else is conspicuous only that it may be shown to be also neglected.

Chapter 8. The Same Rule Holds with Regard to Colours. God's Creatures Generally Not to Be Used, Except for the Purposes to Which He Has Appointed Them

Similarly, too, do even the servants of those barbarians cause the glory to fade from the colours of our garments (by wearing the like); nay, even their party-walls use slightingly, to supply the place of painting, the Tyrian and the violet-coloured and the grand royal hangings, which you laboriously undo and metamorphose. Purple with them is more paltry than red ochre; (and justly,) for what legitimate honour can garments derive from adulteration with illegitimate colours? That which He Himself has not produced is not pleasing to God, unless He was unable to order sheep to be born with purple and sky-blue fleeces! If He was able, then plainly He was unwilling: what God willed not, of course ought not to be fashioned. Those things, then, are not the best by nature which are not from God, the Author of nature. Thus they are understood to be from the devil, from the corrupter of nature: for there is no other whose they can be, if they are not God's; because what are not God's must necessarily be His rival's. But, beside the devil and his angels, other rival of God there is none. Again, if the material substances are of God, it does not immediately follow that such ways of enjoying them among men (are so too). It is matter for inquiry not only whence come conchs, but what sphere of embellishment is assigned them, and where it is that they exhibit their beauty. For all those profane pleasures of worldly shows— as we have already published a volume of their own about them — (ay, and) even idolatry itself, derive their material causes from the creatures of God. Yet a Christian ought not to attach himself to the frenzies of the racecourse, or the atrocities of the arena, or the turpitudes of the stage, simply because God has given to man the horse, and the panther, and the power of speech: just as a Christian cannot commit idolatry with impunity either, because the incense, and the wine, and the fire which feeds (thereon), and the animals which are made the victims, are God's workmanship; since even the material thing which is adored is God's (creature). Thus then, too, with regard to their active use, does the origin of the material substances, which descends from God, excuse (that use) as foreign to God, as guilty forsooth of worldly glory!

Chapter 9. God's Distribution Must Regulate Our Desires, Otherwise We Become the Prey of Ambition and Its Attendant Evils

For, as some particular things distributed by God over certain individual lands, and some one particular tract of sea, are mutually foreign one to the other, they are reciprocally either neglected or desired: (desired) among foreigners, as being rarities; neglected (rightly), if anywhere, among their own compatriots, because in them there is no such fervid longing for a glory which, among its own home-folk, is frigid. But, however, the rareness and outlandishness which arise out of that distribution of possessions which God has ordered as He willed, ever finding favour in the eyes of strangers, excites, from the simple fact of not having what God has made native to other places, the concupiscence of having it. Hence is educed another vice— that of immoderate having; because although, perhaps, having may be permissible, still a limit is bound (to be observed). This (second vice) will be ambition; and hence, too, its name is to be interpreted, in that from concupiscence ambient in the mind it is born, with a view to the desire of glory—a grand desire, forsooth, which (as we have said) is recommended neither by nature nor by truth, but by a vicious passion of the mind—(namely,) concupiscence. And there are other vices connected with ambition and glory. Thus they have withal enhanced the cost of things, in order that (thereby) they might add fuel to themselves also; for concupiscence becomes proportionably greater as it has set a higher value upon the thing which it has eagerly desired. From the smallest caskets is produced an ample patrimony. On a single thread is suspended a million of sesterces. One delicate neck carries about it forests and islands. The slender lobes of the ears exhaust a fortune; and the left hand, with its every finger, sports with a several money-bag. Such is the strength of ambition— (equal) to bearing on one small body, and that a woman's, the product of so copious wealth.

Book II
Chapter 1. Introduction. Modesty to Be Observed Not Only in Its Essence, But in Its Accessories

Handmaids of the living God, my fellow-servants and sisters, the right which I enjoy with you— I, the most meanest in that right of fellow-servantship and brotherhood— emboldens me to address to you a discourse, not, of course, of affection, but paving the way for affection in the cause of your salvation. That salvation— and not (the salvation) of women only, but likewise of men— consists in the exhibition principally of modesty. For since, by the introduction into an appropriation (in) us of the Holy Spirit, we are all "the temple of God," Modesty is the sacristan and priestess of that temple, who is to suffer nothing unclean or profane to be introduced (into it), for fear that the God who inhabits it should be offended, and quite forsake the polluted abode. But on the present occasion we (are to speak) not about modesty, for the enjoining and exacting of which the divine precepts which press (upon us) on every side are sufficient; but about the matters which pertain to it, that is, the manner in which it behooves you to walk. For most women (which very thing I trust God may permit me, with a view, of course, to my own personal censure, to censure in all), either from simple ignorance or else from dissimulation, have the hardihood so to walk as if modesty consisted only in the (bare) integrity of the flesh, and in turning away from (actual) fornication; and there were no need for anything extrinsic to boot— in the matter (I mean) of the arrangement of dress and ornament, the studied graces of form and brilliance:— wearing in their gait the self-same appearance as the women of the nations, from whom the sense of true modesty is absent, because in those who know not God, the Guardian and Master of truth, there is nothing true. For if any modesty can be believed (to exist) in Gentiles, it is plain that it must be imperfect and undisciplined to such a degree that, although it be actively tenacious of itself in the mind up to a certain point, it yet allows itself to relax into licentious extravagances of attire; just in accordance with Gentile perversity, in craving after that of which it carefully shuns the effect. How many a one, in short, is there who does not earnestly desire even to look pleasing to strangers? Who does not on that very account take care to have herself painted out, and denies that she has (ever) been an object of (carnal) appetite? And yet, granting that even this is a practice familiar to Gentile modesty— (namely,) not actually to commit the sin, but still to be willing to do so; or even not to be willing, yet still not quite to refuse— what wonder? For all things which are not God's are perverse. Let those women therefore look to it, who, by not holding fast the whole good, easily mingle with evil even what they do hold fast. Necessary it is that you turn aside from them, as in all other things, so also in your gait; since you ought to be "perfect, as (is) your Father who is in the heavens."

Chapter 2. Perfect Modesty Will Abstain from Whatever Tends to Sin, as Well as from Sin Itself. Difference Between Trust and Presumption. If Secure Ourselves, We Must Not Put Temptation in the Way of Others. We Must Love Our Neighbour as Ourself

You must know that in the eye of perfect, that is, Christian, modesty, (carnal) desire of one's self (on the part of others) is not only not to be desired, but even execrated, by you: first, because the study of making personal grace (which we know to be naturally the inviter of lust) a mean of pleasing does not spring from a sound conscience: why therefore excite toward yourself that evil (passion)? Why invite (that) to which you profess yourself a stranger? Secondly, because we ought not to open a way to temptations, which, by their instancy, sometimes achieve (a wickedness) which God expels from them who are His; (or,) at all events, put the spirit into a thorough tumult by (presenting) a stumbling-block (to it). We ought indeed to walk so holily, and with so entire substantiality of faith, as to be confident and secure in regard of our own conscience, desiring that that (gift) may abide in us to the end, yet not presuming (that it will). For he who presumes feels less apprehension; he who feels less apprehension takes less precaution; he who takes less precaution runs more risk. Fear is the foundation of salvation; presumption is an impediment to fear. More useful, then, is it to apprehend that we may possibly fail, than to presume that we cannot; for apprehending will lead us to fear, fearing to caution, and caution to salvation. On the other hand, if we presume, there will be neither fear nor caution to save us. He who acts securely, and not at the same time warily, possesses no safe and firm security; whereas he who is wary will be truly able to be secure. For His own servants, may the Lord by His mercy take care that to them it may be lawful even to presume on His goodness! But why are we a (source of) danger to our neighbour? Why do we import concupiscence into our neighbour? Which concupiscence, if God, in "amplifying the law," do not dissociate in (the way of) penalty from the actual commission of fornication, I know not whether He allows impunity to him who has been the cause of perdition to some other. For that other, as soon as he has felt concupiscence after your beauty, and has mentally already committed (the deed) which his concupiscence pointed to, perishes; and you have been made the sword which destroys him: so that, albeit you be free from the (actual) crime, you are not free from the odium (attaching to it); as, when a robbery has been committed on some man's estate, the (actual) crime indeed will not be laid to the owner's charge, while yet the domain is branded with ignominy, (and) the owner himself aspersed with the infamy. Are we to paint ourselves out that our neighbours may perish? Where, then, is (the command), "You shall love your neighbour as yourself?" "Care not merely about your own (things), but (about your) neighbour's?" No enunciation of the Holy Spirit ought to be (confined) to the subject immediately in hand merely, and not applied and carried out with a view to every occasion to which its application is useful. Since, therefore, both our own interest and that of others is implicated in the studious pursuit of most perilous (outward) comeliness, it is time for you to know that not merely must the pageantry of fictitious and elaborate beauty be rejected by you; but that of even natural grace must be obliterated by concealment and negligence, as equally dangerous to the glances of (the beholder's) eyes. For, albeit comeliness is not to be censured, as being a bodily happiness, as being an additional outlay of the divine plastic art, as being a kind of goodly garment of the soul; yet it is to be feared, just on account of the injuriousness and violence of suitors: which (injuriousness and violence) even the father of the faith, Abraham, greatly feared in regard of his own wife's grace; and Isaac, by falsely representing Rebecca as his sister, purchased safety by insult!

Chapter 3. Grant that Beauty Be Not to Be Feared: Still It is to Be Shunned as Unnecessary and Vainglorious

Let it now be granted that excellence of form be not to be feared, as neither troublesome to its possessors, nor destructive to its desirers, nor perilous to its compartners; let it be thought (to be) not exposed to temptations, not surrounded by stumbling-blocks: it is enough that to angels of God it is not necessary. For, where modesty is, there beauty is idle; because properly the use and fruit of beauty is voluptuousness, unless any one thinks that there is some other harvest for bodily grace to reap. Are women who think that, in furnishing to their neighbour that which is demanded of beauty, they are furnishing it to themselves also, to augment that (beauty) when (naturally) given them, and to strive after it when not (thus) given? Some one will say, "Why, then, if voluptuousness be shut out and chastity let in, may (we) not enjoy the praise of beauty alone, and glory in a bodily good?" Let whoever finds pleasure in "glorying in the flesh" see to that. To us in the first place, there is no studious pursuit of "glory," because "glory" is the essence of exaltation. Now exaltation is incongruous for professors of humility according to God's precepts. Secondly, if all "glory" is "vain" and insensate, how much more (glory) in the flesh, especially to us? For even if "glorying" is (allowable), we ought to wish our sphere of pleasing to lie in the graces of the Spirit, not in the flesh; because we are "suitors" of things spiritual. In those things wherein our sphere of labour lies, let our joy lie. From the sources whence we hope for salvation, let us cull our "glory." Plainly, a Christian will "glory" even in the flesh; but (it will be) when it has endured laceration for Christ's sake, in order that the spirit may be crowned in it, not in order that it may draw the eyes and sighs of youths after it. Thus (a thing) which, from whatever point you look at it, is in your case superfluous, you may justly disdain if you have it not, and neglect if you have. Let a holy woman, if naturally beautiful, give none so great occasion (for carnal appetite). Certainly, if even she be so, she ought not to set off (her beauty), but even to obscure it.

Chapter 4. Concerning the Plea of "Pleasing the Husband."

As if I were speaking to Gentiles, addressing you with a Gentile precept, and (one which is) common to all, (I would say,) "You are bound to please your husbands only." But you will please them in proportion as you take no care to please others. Be without carefulness, blessed (sisters): no wife is "ugly" to her own husband. She "pleased" him enough when she was selected (by him as his wife); whether commended by form or by character. Let none of you think that, if she abstain from the care of her person, she will incur the hatred and aversion of husbands. Every husband is the exactor of chastity; but beauty, a believing (husband) does not require, because we are not captivated by the same graces which the Gentiles think (to be) graces: an unbelieving one, on the other hand, even regards with suspicion, just from that infamous opinion of us which the Gentiles have. For whom, then, is it that you cherish your beauty? If for a believer, he does not exact it: if for an unbeliever, he does not believe in it unless it be artless. Why are you eager to please either one who is suspicious, or else one who desires it not?

Chapter 5. Some Refinements in Dress and Personal Appearance Lawful, Some Unlawful. Pigments Come Under the Latter Head

These suggestions are not made to you, of course, to be developed into an entire crudity and wildness of appearance; nor are we seeking to persuade you of the good of squalor and slovenliness; but of the limit and norm and just measure of cultivation of the person. There must be no overstepping of that line to which simple and sufficient refinements limit their desires— that line which is pleasing to God. For they who rub their skin with medicaments, stain their cheeks with rouge, make their eyes prominent with antimony, sin against Him . To them, I suppose, the plastic skill of God is displeasing! In their own persons, I suppose, they convict, they censure, the Artificer of all things! For censure they do when they amend, when they add to, (His work;) taking these their additions, of course, from the adversary artificer. That adversary artificer is the devil. For who would show the way to change the body, but he who by wickedness transfigured man's spirit? He it is, undoubtedly, who adapted ingenious devices of this kind; that in your persons it may be apparent that you, in a certain sense, do violence to God. Whatever is born is the work of God. Whatever, then, is plastered on (that), is the devil's work. To superinduce on a divine work Satan's ingenuities, how criminal is it! Our servants borrow nothing from our personal enemies: soldiers eagerly desire nothing from the foes of their own general; for, to demand for (your own) use anything from the adversary of Him in whose hand you are, is a transgression. Shall a Christian be assisted in anything by that evil one? (If he do,) I know not whether this name (of "Christian") will continue (to belong) to him; for he will be his in whose lore he eagerly desires to be instructed. But how alien from your schoolings and professions are (these things)! How unworthy the Christian name, to wear a fictitious face, (you,) on whom simplicity in every form is enjoined!— to lie in your appearance, (you,) to whom (lying) with the tongue is not lawful!— to seek after what is another's, (you,) to whom is delivered (the precept of) abstinence from what is another's!— to practise adultery in your mien, (you,) who make modesty your study! Think, blessed (sisters), how will you keep God's precepts if you shall not keep in your own persons His lineaments?

Chapter 6. Of Dyeing the Hair

I see some (women) turn (the colour of) their hair with saffron. They are ashamed even of their own nation, (ashamed) that their procreation did not assign them to Germany and to Gaul: thus, as it is, they transfer their hair (there)! Ill, ay, most ill, do they augur for themselves with their flame-coloured head, and think that graceful which (in fact) they are polluting! Nay, moreover, the force of the cosmetics burns ruin into the hair; and the constant application of even any undrugged moisture, lays up a store of harm for the head; while the sun's warmth, too, so desirable for imparting to the hair at once growth and dryness, is hurtful. What "grace" is compatible with "injury?" What "beauty" with "impurities?" Shall a Christian woman heap saffron on her head, as upon an altar? For, whatever is wont to be burned to the honour of the unclean spirit, that— unless it is applied for honest, and necessary, and salutary uses, for which God's creature was provided— may seem to be a sacrifice. But, however, God says, "Which of you can make a white hair black, or out of a black a white?" And so they refute the Lord! "Behold!" say they, "instead of white or black, we make it yellow—more winning in grace." And yet such as repent of having lived to old age do attempt to change it even from white to black! O temerity! The age which is the object of our wishes and prayers blushes (for itself)! A theft is effected! Youth, wherein we have sinned, is sighed after! The opportunity of sobriety is spoiled! Far from Wisdom's daughters be folly so great! The more old age tries to conceal itself, the more will it be detected. Here is a veritable eternity, in the (perennial) youth of your head! Here we have an "incorruptibility" to "put on," with a view to the new house of the Lord which the divine monarchy promises! Well do you speed toward the Lord; well do you hasten to be quit of this most iniquitous world, to whom it is unsightly to approach (your own) end!

Chapter 7. Of Elaborate Dressing of the Hair in Other Ways, and Its Bearing Upon Salvation

What service, again, does all the labour spent in arranging the hair render to salvation? Why is no rest allowed to your hair, which must now be bound, now loosed, now cultivated, now thinned out? Some are anxious to force their hair into curls, some to let it hang loose and flying; not with good simplicity: beside which, you affix I know not what enormities of subtle and textile perukes; now, after the manner of a helmet of undressed hide, as it were a sheath for the head and a covering for the crown; now, a mass (drawn) backward toward the neck. The wonder is, that there is no (open) contending against the Lord's prescripts! It has been pronounced that no one can add to his own stature. You, however, do add to your weight some kind of rolls, or shield-bosses, to be piled upon your necks! If you feel no shame at the enormity, feel some at the pollution; for fear you may be fitting on a holy and Christian head the slough of some one else's head, unclean perchance, guilty perchance and destined to hell. Nay, rather banish quite away from your "free" head all this slavery of ornamentation. In vain do you labour to seem adorned: in vain do you call in the aid of all the most skilful manufacturers of false hair. God bids you "be veiled." I believe (He does so) for fear the heads of some should be seen! And oh that in "that day" of Christian exultation, I, most miserable (as I am), may elevate my head, even though below (the level of) your heels! I shall (then) see whether you will rise with (your) ceruse and rouge and saffron, and in all that parade of headgear: whether it will be women thus tricked out whom the angels carry up to meet Christ in the air! If these (decorations) are now good, and of God, they will then also present themselves to the rising bodies, and will recognise their several places. But nothing can rise except flesh and spirit sole and pure. Whatever, therefore, does not rise in (the form of) spirit and flesh is condemned, because it is not of God. From things which are condemned abstain, even at the present day. At the present day let God see you such as He will see you then.

Chapter 8. Men Not Excluded from These Remarks on Personal Adornment

Of course, now, I, a man, as being envious of women, am banishing them quite from their own (domains). Are there, in our case too, some things which, in respect of the sobriety we are to maintain on account of the fear due to God, are disallowed? If it is true, (as it is,) that in men, for the sake of women (just as in women for the sake of men), there is implanted, by a defect of nature, the will to please; and if this sex of ours acknowledges to itself deceptive trickeries of form peculiarly its own—(such as) to cut the beard too sharply; to pluck it out here and there; to shave round about (the mouth); to arrange the hair, and disguise its hoariness by dyes; to remove all the incipient down all over the body; to fix (each particular hair) in its place with (some) womanly pigment; to smooth all the rest of the body by the aid of some rough powder or other: then, further, to take every opportunity for consulting the mirror; to gaze anxiously into it:— while yet, when (once) the knowledge of God has put an end to all wish to please by means of voluptuous attraction, all these things are rejected as frivolous, as hostile to modesty. For where God is, there modesty is; there is sobriety her assistant and ally. How, then, shall we practise modesty without her instrumental mean, that is, without sobriety? How, moreover, shall we bring sobriety to bear on the discharge of (the functions of) modesty, unless seriousness in appearance and in countenance, and in the general aspect of the entire man, mark our carriage?

Chapter 9. Excess in Dress, as Well as in Personal Culture, to Be Shunned. Arguments Drawn from I Cor. VII.

Wherefore, with regard to clothing also, and all the remaining lumber of your self-elaboration, the like pruning off and retrenchment of too redundant splendour must be the object of your care. For what boots it to exhibit in your face temperance and unaffectedness, and a simplicity altogether worthy of the divine discipline, but to invest all the other parts of the body with the luxurious absurdities of pomps and delicacies? How intimate is the connection which these pomps have with the business of voluptuousness, and how they interfere with modesty, is easily discernible from the fact that it is by the allied aid of dress that they prostitute the grace of personal comeliness: so plain is it that if (the pomps) be wanting, they render (that grace) bootless and thankless, as if it were disarmed and wrecked. On the other hand, if natural beauty fails, the supporting aid of outward embellishment supplies a grace, as it were, from its own inherent power. Those times of life, in fact, which are at last blest with quiet and withdrawn into the harbour of modesty, the splendour and dignity of dress lure away (from that rest and that harbour), and disquiet seriousness by seductions of appetite, which compensate for the chill of age by the provocative charms of apparel. First, then, blessed (sisters), (take heed) that you admit not to your use meretricious and prostitutionary garbs and garments: and, in the next place, if there are any of you whom the exigencies of riches, or birth, or past dignities, compel to appear in public so gorgeously arrayed as not to appear to have attained wisdom, take heed to temper an evil of this kind; lest, under the pretext of necessity, you give the rein without stint to the indulgence of licence. For how will you be able to fulfil (the requirements of) humility, which our (school) profess, if you do not keep within bounds the enjoyment of your riches and elegancies, which tend so much to "glory?" Now it has ever been the wont of glory to exalt, not to humble. "Why, shall we not use what is our own?" Who prohibits your using it? Yet (it must be) in accordance with the apostle, who warns us "to use this world as if we abuse it not; for the fashion of this world is passing away." And "they who buy are so to act as if they possessed not." Why so? Because he had laid down the premiss, saying, "The time is wound up." If, then he shows plainly that even wives themselves are so to be had as if they be not had, on account of the straits of the times, what would be his sentiments about these vain appliances of theirs? Why, are there not many, withal, who so do, and seal themselves up to eunuchhood for the sake of the kingdom of God, spontaneously relinquishing a pleasure so honourable, and (as we know) permitted? Are there not some who prohibit to themselves (the use of) the very "creature of God," abstaining from wine and animal food, the enjoyments of which border upon no peril or solicitude; but they sacrifice to God the humility of their soul even in the chastened use of food? Sufficiently, therefore, have you, too, used your riches and your delicacies; sufficiently have you cut down the fruits of your dowries, before (receiving) the knowledge of saving disciplines. We are they "upon whom the ends of the ages have met, having ended their course." We have been predestined by God, before the world was, (to arise) in the extreme end of the times. And so we are trained by God for the purpose of chastising, and (so to say) emasculating, the world. We are the circumcision — spiritual and carnal— of all things; for both in the spirit and in the flesh we circumcise worldly principles.

Chapter 10. Tertullian Refers Again to the Question of the Origin of All These Ornaments and Embellishments.

It was God, no doubt, who showed the way to dye wools with the juices of herbs and the humours of conchs! It had escaped Him, when He was bidding the universe to come into being, to issue a command for (the production of) purple and scarlet sheep! It was God, too, who devised by careful thought the manufactures of those very garments which, light and thin (in themselves), were to be heavy in price alone; God who produced such grand implements of gold for confining or parting the hair; God who introduced (the fashion of) finely-cut wounds for the ears, and set so high a value upon the tormenting of His own work and the tortures of innocent infancy, learning to suffer with its earliest breath, in order that from those scars of the body— born for the steel!— should hang I know not what (precious) grains, which, as we may plainly see, the Parthians insert, in place of studs, upon their very shoes! And yet even the gold itself, the "glory" of which carries you away, serves a certain race (so Gentile literature tells us) for chains! So true is it that it is not intrinsic worth, but rarity, which constitutes the goodness (of these things): the excessive labour, moreover, of working them with arts introduced by the means of the sinful angels, who were the revealers withal of the material substances themselves, joined with their rarity, excited their costliness, and hence a lust on the part of women to possess (that) costliness. But, if the self-same angels who disclosed both the material substances of this kind and their charms— of gold, I mean, and lustrous stones— and taught men how to work them, and by and by instructed them, among their other (instructions), in (the virtues of) eyelid-powder and the dyeings of fleeces, have been condemned by God, as Enoch tells us, how shall we please God while we joy in the things of those (angels) who, on these accounts, have provoked the anger and the vengeance of God?

Now, granting that God did foresee these things; that God permitted them; that Esaias finds fault with no garment of purple, represses no coil, reprobates no crescent-shaped neck ornaments; still let us not, as the Gentiles do, flatter ourselves with thinking that God is merely a Creator, not likewise a Downlooker on His own creatures. For how far more usefully and cautiously shall we act, if we hazard the presumption that all these things were indeed provided at the beginning and placed in the world by God, in order that there should now be means of putting to the proof the discipline of His servants, in order that the licence of using should be the means whereby the experimental trials of continence should be conducted? Do not wise heads of families purposely offer and permit some things to their servants in order to try whether and how they will use the things thus permitted; whether (they will do so) with honesty, or with moderation? But how far more praiseworthy (the servant) who abstains entirely; who has a wholesome fear even of his lord's indulgence! Thus, therefore, the apostle too: "All things," says he, "are lawful, but not all are expedient." How much more easily will he fear what is unlawful who has a reverent dread of what is lawful?

Chapter 11. Christian Women, Further, Have Not the Same Causes for Appearing in Public, and Hence for Dressing in Fine Array as Gentiles. On the Contrary, Their Appearance Should Always Distinguish Them from Such

Moreover, what causes have you for appearing in public in excessive grandeur, removed as you are from the occasions which call for such exhibitions? For you neither make the circuit of the temples, nor demand (to be present at) public shows, nor have any acquaintance with the holy days of the Gentiles. Now it is for the sake of all these public gatherings, and of much seeing and being seen, that all pomps (of dress) are exhibited before the public eye; either for the purpose of transacting the trade of voluptuousness, or else of inflating "glory." You, however, have no cause of appearing in public, except such as is serious. Either some brother who is sick is visited, or else the sacrifice is offered, or else the word of God is dispensed. Whichever of these you like to name is a business of sobriety and sanctity, requiring no extraordinary attire, with (studious) arrangement and (wanton) negligence. And if the requirements of Gentile friendships and of kindly offices call you, why not go forth clad in your own armour; (and) all the more, in that (you have to go) to such as are strangers to the faith? So that between the handmaids of God and of the devil there may be a difference; so that you may be an example to them, and they may be edified in you; so that (as the apostle says) "God may be magnified in your body." But magnified He is in the body through modesty: of course, too, through attire suitable to modesty.

Well, but it is urged by some, "Let not the Name be blasphemed in us, if we make any derogatory change from our old style and dress." Let us, then, not abolish our old vices! let us maintain the same character, if we must maintain the same appearance (as before); and then truly the nations will not blaspheme! A grand blasphemy is that by which it is said, "Ever since she became a Christian, she walks in poorer garb!" Will you fear to appear poorer, from the time that you have been made more wealthy; and fouler, from the time when you have been made more clean? Is it according to the decree of Gentiles, or according to the decree of God, that it becomes Christians to walk?

Chapter 12. Such Outward Adornments Meretricious, and Therefore Unsuitable to Modest Women

Let us only wish that we may be no cause for just blasphemy! But how much more provocative of blasphemy is it that you, who are called modesty's priestesses, should appear in public decked and painted out after the manner of the immodest? Else, (if you so do,) what inferiority would the poor unhappy victims of the public lusts have (beneath you)? Whom, albeit some laws were (formerly) wont to restrain them from (the use of) matrimonial and matronly decorations, now, at all events, the daily increasing depravity of the age has raised so nearly to an equality with all the most honourable women, that the difficulty is to distinguish them. And yet, even the Scriptures suggest (to us the reflection), that meretricious attractivenesses of form are invariably conjoined with and appropriate to bodily prostitution. That powerful state which presides over the seven mountains and very many waters, has merited from the Lord the appellation of a prostitute. But what kind of garb is the instrumental mean of her comparison with that appellation? She sits, to be sure, "in purple, and scarlet, and gold, and precious stone." How accursed are the things without (the aid of) which an accursed prostitute could not have been described! It was the fact that Thamar "had painted out and adorned herself" that led Judah to regard her as a harlot, and thus, because she was hidden beneath her "veil,"— the quality of her garb belying her as if she had been a harlot—he judged (her to be one), and addressed and bargained with (her as such). Whence we gather an additional confirmation of the lesson, that provision must be made in every way against all immodest associations and suspicions. For why is the integrity of a chaste mind defiled by its neighbour's suspicion? Why is a thing from which I am averse hoped for in me? Why does not my garb pre-announce my character, to prevent my spirit from being wounded by shamelessness through (the channel of) my ears? Grant that it be lawful to assume the appearance of a modest woman: to assume that of an immodest is, at all events, not lawful.

Chapter 13. It is Not Enough that God Know Us to Be Chaste: We Must Seem So Before Men. Especially in These Times of Persecution We Must Inure Our Bodies to the Hardships Which They May Not Improbably Be Called to Suffer

Perhaps some (woman) will say: "To me it is not necessary to be approved by men; for I do not require the testimony of men: God is the inspector of the heart." (That) we all know; provided, however, we remember what the same (God) has said through the apostle: "Let your probity appear before men." For what purpose, except that malice may have no access at all to you, or that you may be an example and testimony to the evil? Else, what is (that): "Let your works shine?" Why, moreover, does the Lord call us the light of the world; why has He compared us to a city built upon a mountain; if we do not shine in (the midst of) darkness, and stand eminent amid them who are sunk down? If you hide your lamp beneath a bushel, you must necessarily be left quite in darkness, and be run against by many. The things which make us luminaries of the world are these— our good works. What is good, moreover, provided it be true and full, loves not darkness: it joys in being seen, and exults over the very pointings which are made at it. To Christian modesty it is not enough to be so, but to seem so too. For so great ought its plenitude to be, that it may flow out from the mind to the garb, and burst out from the conscience to the outward appearance; so that even from the outside it may gaze, as it were, upon its own furniture, — (a furniture) such as to be suited to retain faith as its inmate perpetually. For such delicacies as tend by their softness and effeminacy to unman the manliness of faith are to be discarded. Otherwise, I know not whether the wrist that has been wont to be surrounded with the palmleaf-like bracelet will endure till it grow into the numb hardness of its own chain! I know not whether the leg that has rejoiced in the anklet will suffer itself to be squeezed into the gyve! I fear the neck, beset with pearl and emerald nooses, will give no room to the broadsword! Wherefore, blessed (sisters), let us meditate on hardships, and we shall not feel them; let us abandon luxuries, and we shall not regret them. Let us stand ready to endure every violence, having nothing which we may fear to leave behind. It is these things which are the bonds which retard our hope. Let us cast away earthly ornaments if we desire heavenly. Love not gold; in which (one substance) are branded all the sins of the people of Israel. You ought to hate what ruined your fathers; what was adored by them who were forsaking God. Even then (we find) gold is food for the fire. But Christians always, and now more than ever, pass their times not in gold but in iron: the stoles of martyrdom are (now) preparing: the angels who are to carry us are (now) being awaited! Do you go forth (to meet them) already arrayed in the cosmetics and ornaments of prophets and apostles; drawing your whiteness from simplicity, your ruddy hue from modesty; painting your eyes with bashfulness, and your mouth with silence; implanting in your ears the words of God; fitting on your necks the yoke of Christ. Submit your head to your husbands, and you will be enough adorned. Busy your hands with spinning; keep your feet at home; and you will "please" better than (by arraying yourselves) in gold. Clothe yourselves with the silk of uprightness, the fine linen of holiness, the purple of modesty. Thus painted, you will have God as your Lover!